W9-CXS-431

Shortcuts on Wine

SHORTCUTS ON WINE

EDMOND MASCIANA

CAPRA PRESS

SANTA BARABARA

To Jon,
the best son in the world,
and Ginger,
the best sweetheart in the world.

Cover design, book design, typography and interior illustrations
by Frank Goad, Santa Barbara, CA

LIBRARY OF CONGRESS CATALOGING-IN-PUBLICATION DATA

Masciana, Edmond.
　　Shot cuts on wine : everything the wine lover needs to know /
Edmond Masciana
　　　p. cm.
　　Includes index.
　　ISBN 0-88496-404-3 (paper)
　　1. Wine and wine making. I. Title.
TP548.M383　1996
641.2'2—dc20　　　　　　　　　　　　　96-10634
　　　　　　　　　　　　　　　　　　　　　　CIP

CAPRA 🐏 PRESS
Post Office Box 2068
Santa Barbara, CA 93120

TABLE OF CONTENTS

FOREWORD

$\mathcal{S}$INCE 1984, when I began teaching wine courses for the South Bay Adult School in Manhattan Beach, California, the question asked by students more than any other was, "What book can you recommend that will outline the basics like you've done in this class?"

Although I've probably read at least half of all the wine books ever written, I was stumped for an answer. As I continued to teach classes there and through the UCLA Extension program and El Camino College Adult programs, that same question kept cropping up. And, I still had the same answer.

So, in 1988, I decided to write one. This book is dedicated to the thousands of students who have taken my wine classes in the past and will take wine classes in the future. I have tried to address as many topics as the beginning wine lover would be interested in and a few he may not. It is structured in the same manner as the beginning wine class I've taught for many years.

At the end of this book are my suggestions for other books to read if you want to increase your knowledge in one or more specific areas of wine. I encourage you to do so. Wine is a wonderful topic, not to mention a wonderful drink. It is pleasing to the eyes, nose and mouth. The story of wine from economic, religious, cultural and political viewpoints is quite fascinating. Wine has been an integral part of man's life for over 8,000 years. Hopefully, without interference from neo-prohibitionists, it will survive another 8,000 years.

Cheers,
ED MASCIANA
February, 1996

INTRODUCTION

*I*T'S HARD TO IMAGINE that the second world war jump-started America's interest in wine. At the very least, it had an effect. Many of the baby boomers' fathers were stationed in Europe during World War II and became exposed to the European view of food and wine. The meal was a family affair. Work stopped, friends and family gathered to enjoy the sensuous pleasures of fresh food and local wine. Once exposed to this form of dining, it's hard to go back to a bologna sandwich and a beer.

In most European homes wine is a natural and normal part of a meal. That is not yet the case in the United States, although we are slowly ridding ourselves of the social taboos of drinking wine with a meal. Most American wine drinkers are affluent. Most are college educated and active. One major appeal of wine is that, with its moderate alcohol content, it is an alternative to the cocktail. White wine seems to have replaced hard liquor as the cocktail of choice, possibly because of its flavor, chillability, lightness and, often, slight sweetness. This condition is hopefully a prelude to consuming wine with food. However, it must be pointed out that imbibing any alcohol, even wine, on an empty stomach is like playing with matches in an oil refinery.

Wine with Food

Wine tastes good, and its myriad of flavors are compatible with a variety of foods. Wine enhances food, and it is also life-enhancing. With regard to the latter, wine is now served in hospitals, has been proven to be highly beneficial in geriatrics and often is prescribed by modern doctors, as was the case centuries ago, in the treatment of many diseases, especially heart disease.

Wine, unlike other beverages, actually complements food and food complements wine. Your most sensitive taste sensor is the tongue. It is made up of thousands of tiny taste buds shaped like a mushroom; a stem with a cap which overhangs on top. As you eat, your taste buds trap food between the stem and the cap, blotting out the bud's ability to taste. Your taste buds get overloaded and thus, the food seems to lose its flavor. Wine's naturally high acidity cleanses those taste buds better than anything else. Wines referred to as "food wines" tend to have a higher acidity making them too tart to drink on their own. That acidity cleanses the palate and prepares it to accept the next bite of food.

Acidity curls the tongue and induces you to salivate. The saliva is a natural digestive helping to move the food through the body. Wine is the catalyst in not just enjoying the taste of food but helping to digest it as well. Acidity can work in the opposite direction, too. If you continue to taste a high acid wine without food, your taste buds will become overloaded with acid and your tongue will feel dry and unpleasant. That's why wines with lower acid and/or a touch of sugar are sometimes referred to as "cocktail wines" as they can be consumed without food and not overload the taste buds with acid. Unfortunately, as noted above, this condition forces you to drink wine without the benefit of food, introducing alcohol into the bloodstream twice as fast as if you had had something to eat.

WINE'S HISTORY

The use of wine is cited several times in the Bible, making it one of the most ancient of beverages. It existed in Russia and Mesopotamia at least 7,000 years ago and was probably man's first introduction to alcohol. It endured because it was high enough in alcohol to keep without refrigeration or proper enclosures. Alcohol and sugar are natural preservatives. That's why the first wines were high in alcohol and sweet. They tasted better for a longer period of time.

There are numerous references to wine in the Bible. Noah planted vineyards and "became drunken" according to Genesis IX. Even then, drunkenness was frowned upon. And, of course, there is Jesus' turning of water into wine in the New Testament.

In Western civilization, wine grapes were first cultivated in the Near East around the Mediterranean Basin. The vine and wine culture were first spread by the Greeks into France and Italy (tough news for the French and Italians!). The Greeks called Italy Enotria, "The Land of Staked Vines." Grapes were grown wild in Italy, whereas the Greeks were more scientific. The Italian wine tasted better because the grapes were grown higher off the ground (trained around olive trees), allowing more sunlight to reach them. This ripened the grapes more than those of other countries thus making them more flavorful. The Greeks took this idea of training the vines off the ground to garner more sunlight (referred to as trellising) along with their own practices regarding irrigation and hillside exposures and planted grapes in the further reaches of Europe.

While it was the Greeks who really started the ball rolling, it was certainly the Romans who carried it. They planted vines in every country they conquered and probably a few they didn't. As the Roman Empire expanded, wine grapes were established in nearly every part of present-day Europe.

Vineyards in France, Italy and Germany were extensive by the Middle Ages. The literature of the times clearly shows wine was a staple of life. Coincidentally, wine shares a few properties with two staples, cheese and bread. All are the result of fermentation of one kind or another.

The grape varieties cultivated in Europe today belong to a special species known as *Vitis Vinifera*, meaning winebearer. It numbers well over 5,000 varieties, but only about 100 to 200 are of importance to commercial winemakers. The vinifera grape varieties have been successfully transplanted to many regions besides Europe: Australia, South America, South Africa, New Zealand, Washington, Oregon, California and several other parts of the United States.

CHAPTER 1

VINES: THE KEY TO QUALITY

*T*HERE IS AN OLD VINTNER'S SAYING that great wines are "grown" in the vineyards. It is important then, in the learning of wine, to first grasp the importance of the raw material. In this case the grapes. No winemaker can "create" quality. The winemaker's duty is to take the grapes Nature provides and guide them on their course toward becoming wine. If you begin with the best grapes and employ great skill and experience, you have the potential to make great wine. The term here is "potential." There is an old axiom among winemakers, "You can make poor wine from fine grapes, but you can't make fine wine from poor grapes."

Nearly all of the world's vines are a combination of American, *Vitis Labrusca*, rootstocks to which have been grafted the so-called "noble" grapes of *Vitis Vinifera* varietals, such as Cabernet Sauvignon, Chardonnay and Riesling. Originally all vines were grown on their original rootstock. Unfortunately, this rootstock is susceptible to a louse called phylloxera which literally eats the plant from the tip of the root up. We will discuss this topic in another chapter.

In order to make the best wine from each grapevine,

many factors must be taken into consideration. The French call it *terroir*, which means the ecosystem of the vineyard. It comprises all the factors making the vineyard unique: soil composition, slope, temperature and rainfall at certain times during the maturation of the grapes, drainage, etc. Once the grapes are harvested, their potential has already been set.

The soil the vines are planted in is of paramount importance to the quality of the grapes. The red "terra rossa" soil, high in iron oxide and common to parts of the Napa Valley, Eastern Washington and the Sierra foothills, has been responsible, to some extent, for the hearty Cabernet Sauvignons produced in those regions. High granite soil-found in Bordeaux and Italy produces a different but no less desirable grape. The very light, chalk-like and nearly white soil found in several areas of Sonoma, the Central Coast and Oregon has been proven to be ideal for Pinot Noir and Chardonnay. Riesling seems to like soils where roughly half the composition is stones and gravel.

Such viticultural intricacies have been known in Europe for centuries since, by trial and error, correct locations for specific varietals were found. Where Chardonnay did poorly, Cabernet thrived and vice versa. German red wines, with few exceptions, are light and flavorless. Their Rieslings, the grape that Germany's terrain is best suited for, are beyond reproach. California, with its short history of wine, was aware of these intricacies. Only in recent years, however, have California vintners made large strides in isolating these special *terroirs* in areas where soiland climate conditions are favorable to a specific varietal.

A century of winemaking is a very brief span of time. Once a vine is planted it requires three or four years in the ground before it can bear fruit, and very little at that. Vines do not reach full bearing capacity until they are seven years of age. At such time the viticulturist can make a quality assessment. A red grape may yield a wine that will need to be aged for perhaps three years before the winemaker can make a firm quality assessment.

From the time the vine is planted until the time the final product is analyzed as being superior in quality, seven or more years have elapsed. And, we're only talking about one wine, made from one vintage. It may take three or four vintages to get a "read" on the vineyard. In the meantime, a decade or more has passed. Usually, grapegrowers will have several "experiments" going at the same time (planting a row each of different grape varietals in the same vineyard to see how good the wine made from each can be), thus allowing them to make an evaluation after a few years using many different lots. All the while, however, no wine is sold, no income from these experiments is generated.

CLIMATE: THE CATALYST

Vines, to survive, cannot tolerate either excessive heat or cold. To bear fruit of even ordinary quality, the temperature range is severely limited. For these reasons, viticulture (the growing of wine grapes) exists only in a very narrow range of latitudes worldwide, and then only in areas where soils are suitable.

UC Davis devised a system for measuring ambient temperature during the growing season. It has long been known in Europe that certain grapes thrive better in certain areas than others. The search for suitable climates in California was simplified in the 1960s when professors at the university devised the

"Zone" system for vines.

The minimum ambient temperature during the growing season when vines can be cultivated is 50 degrees Fahrenheit. The Zone system is based on heat summation expressed as "degree days." Degree days simply means that if the high temperature on a certain day is 70° F. and the low is 50° F., then the average temperature on that day is 60°F. Since the base is 50° F., the heat summation in excess of 50° is 10°. and is expressed as "10 degree days." The total number of degree days experienced in a particular location throughout the entire growing season, roughly March through October or about 200 days, denotes the Zone (sometimes called Region) in which that location falls.

To calculate degree days, you take the average of the difference between 50° and the average temperature for that day. For example, a particular vineyard's 200 day growing season has an average daily temperature of 70°. The temperature is 20° over the base minimum of 50° per day. The important number in the zone system is the average temperature. If the high is 80° and the low is 40°, the average is 60°. The difference between this average and the base (50°) is 10° and is calculated as 10 degree days. The average temperatures change as the season gets warmer. On a day that the high temperature reached 90° and the low 60° the average would be computed as 75° (the average between 60° and 90°) The difference between 50° (the base number) and 75° is 25° so we add 25 degree days to the total. In April, May and June the high temperatures could average 70°. In July, August and September the high temperature could reach over 100°. On a day where the high temperature reaches 100° and the low 60°, we take the average between 60° and 100° which is 80°.

16

80° is 30° higher than 50° (the base number) so we add 30 degree days. At the end of the growing season (harvest day), we add up all the numbers for each day and categorize the vineyard by the following table.

HEAT ZONES

Zone I—2,500 degree days or less

Zone II—2,501 - 3,000 degree days

Zone III—3,001 - 3,500 degree days

Zone IV—3,501 - 4,000 degree days

Zone V—4,001 degree days or more

If the average temperature throughout the growing season is 62°, the difference between that average and our base of 50° is 12. Multiply that by 200 days and you have 2,400 degree days or a Zone I (also referred to as Region I). If the average is 68° the difference between that and the 50° base is 18°. Multiply 18 by 200 days and you have 3,600 degree days or a Region IV. As you can see it doesn't take much change over the growing season to have a dramatic impact on the Zone.

Many sensitive varietals, such as Pinot Noir, thrive best in the cooler climates such as Zone I. Chardonnay prefers a slightly warmer climate found in Zones I and II. Cabernet Sauvignon does best in significantly warmer climates like those found in Zone III. These zones were established after decades of studies were conducted by UC Davis. These studies are now invaluable to viticulturists who wish to plant a specific varietal because they must first locate the correct soil conditions and then determine if the climate is compatible. These studies give them a little more information from which to base an expensive decision on other than pure luck. If the vineyard selection does not meet the criteria for the grape they wish to plant, they must either select another varietal or search for another location, assuming the highest quality grapes are their goal.

The Zone system is only a guide. It only takes into consideration the overall summation of heat in the vineyard and calculates that summation based on the highest temperature reached that day. It doesn't make allowances if a high temperature of 90° was reached for five minutes or five hours. The vines, however, can sure tell the difference.

You would not base a very expensive decision solely on the Zone system with regard to what you would plant and where. Some grapes flower early making them susceptible to early Spring frosts. All the heat in the world won't save a dead grape. Some grapes ripen late, making them susceptible to Fall hailstorms. It's tough to make wine from grapes shot with ice pellets. When the vineyard warms, when it cools, how hot it gets, its rain patterns, etc. are all very important considerations. The Zone system is a guide addressing only one of these concerns, the summation of heat in the vineyard. For this reason it is only a guide, not the whole enchillada.

Microclimates; are small sections of larger areas which, due to some natural circumstance like proximity to a lake or hill or open to sea breezes, consistently provide climatic conditions different from the Zone they are located in. Therefore, a Zone II region might contain a small Zone I or Zone III within its boundaries. Microclimates can be as large as several miles in area, or as small as half a city block.

Vines reach full bearing age in about seven years. For approximately the next 30-40 years they will sustain full yields as long as they are not ravaged by disease. For fine wine varietals, crops are decided upon in tons of grapes harvested per acre of vines. This averages between three and seven tons per acre. The fluctuation depends on the varietal and the methods of pruning, watering, fertilizing and other actions affecting vine growth. At 50 years of age the production of fruit by the vine gradually declines. At 60-70 years old it will produce less than half the quantity of fruit (though often times very intense) of its younger years. At this point you are getting half as much wine as you once did. Most likely you can't charge twice as much to make up for the lost yield. This is why vines are replaced about every 50 years, even though they can live to well over a century.

A vine's yearly cycle begins early in Spring, usually the first week of March. Since vines are deciduous, like many trees, they are dormant and without leaves in winter. With the first warming of the weather, sap, stored in the vine's root system, rises through the vine trunk and upward to its branches, called "canes." The length of these canes is controlled by viticulturists by pruning (cutting back) the vine during its dormant period. On each cane are many tiny nodules, called "buds," from which new growth is generated.

By controlling the number of buds on each cane through pruning, the viticulturist can control the number of grape clusters generated. This will affect the final yield of the grapes. To grow great Chardonnay grapes, it is generally thought that a yield of three to four tons per acre is desirable (although new techniques are allowing premium quality grapes to be grown at higher yields). Lower yields are achieved by cutting off grape clusters before they mature. This is referred to as leaf thinning. If left alone, the vineyard would produce seven to nine tons per acre of very ordinary, flavorless grapes from which you would make ordinary, flavorless wine. The root system can only provide so much nutrients to the grape clusters. Generally speaking, each cluster will get its share as long as there aren't too many others on the vine in competition with it.

The sap rises, and the pressure increases. This forces the buds to swell until their protective cover splits and the first tiny leaf and floral cluster emerges. This is called "bud break." The "shoot" of new growth containing the first leaf, the floral cluster and additional tiny leaves, then grows at a very fast pace, as much as six inches per day, forming new canes. Each cane, with its supporting leaves, will bear one or two bunches of grapes.

The cluster is actually a tiny flower pod which, when developed, will pop its cap and release a tiny flower. Since vines are hermaphroditic, or self-pollinating, each flower contains both the male and female elements for pollination which is accomplished by gentle wind movements during early morning hours.

When the flower emerges, the vine has "bloomed." Pollination then takes place over a period of about 10 days and is so delicate that any rain, high wind or even an extreme in temperature will prevent complete pollination and fruit development. As with each phase of winemaking, a delicate balance is critical. A gentle breeze is needed to carry pollination through its cycle. A lot of wind will be destructive, missing enough vines to where pollination will be sporadic and not each vine will produce.

After pollination, called a "set" the vines then transform their flowers to miniature grapes, one of the great wonders of nature. The green, buckshot-sized grapes, each of which is called a "berry," then enlarge rapidly in size, doubling in June and again in July. By the end of July or early

August, in red wine grapes, a blush of color begins to occur, called *veraison*, a French word for color development as the grapes grow toward maturity.

These new vine canes, leaves and floral clusters are extremely delicate. The possibility of frost and freezing temperatures is a major threat, and if severe enough, can destroy the entire crop. Vineyardists use a variety of frost protection equipment (fans, heaters or even helicopters) during cold snaps to combat this threat. April is the worst month in terms of the possibility of frost damage. By May, the new canes have a length of three feet or more. The floral clusters at this stage look like miniature grape clusters with green "grapes" about the size of buckshot. These "grapes" are mostly made up of acid. Through the process of photosynthesis, the sun's rays transform that acid into sugar.

Depending upon the varietal, maturity will be reached between early September and the end of October. As the grapes ripen, their total fruit acid content decreases proportionally as their sugar content increases. When the balance between these two is correct in the view of the winemaker, the grapes will be harvested.

Grapes generally ripen in an orderly and predetermined pattern. Some reach maturity at the beginning of the harvest season (early varietals), others toward the middle of the harvest season (mid-ripening varietals), and the remainder at the end of the harvest (late-ripening varietals). Early varietals include Pinot Noir and Chardonnay. Mid-ripening varietals include Sauvignon Blanc and Barbera. Of the late-ripening varietals, Cabernet Sauvignon, Zinfandel and Riesling are usually the last to be harvested.

Sugar development in grapes is measured by winemakers in "degrees Brix," or percentage of sugar by weight.

Grapes picked at 22.5 Brix contain 22.5% sugar. Acid is measured by volume and expressed as a percentage. A balanced Chardonnay might be picked at "22.5 Brix with .75% acid," a fine balance in Cabernet Sauvignon could be "23.5 Brix with .65% acid." These two figures refer to the balance of the grapes at harvest and prior to fermentation. After grapes are fermented into wine, a different measurement system is used.

Too often, however, a quality assessment of the grapes is done "by the numbers." These figures are only a guide to the quality of the grapes. The most important factor is grape maturity, and this can only be determined by an experienced vineyardist. Maturity refers to the complex acids, fruit components and essences which make wine so different from other beverages and contributes to the myriad of flavors one enjoys. Maturity is attained when all these components are in the grape and will be present in the finished wine. It is unmeasurable. It is determined through experience both of the winemaker and the grapegrower, oftentimes just by tasting the grapes before harvest.

Another frequently used word to determine wine balance is expressed by the symbol "pH." This term is chemical shorthand for measurement of the acids; contained in the total acid structure of a wine. A liquid that is neutral, that is neither acid nor alkaline base, would have a pH value of seven. Higher numbers indicate a higher base, or alkaline solution, while lower numbers indicate increasing acid. The pH value of fine wine generally ranges from 3.0 to 3.7, usually lower in white wines than reds. In white wines, a lower (better) pH will give the wine a very "crisp" taste. In red wines, a lower pH will affect its ageability and flavor.

Active acids, such as malic (found in green apples), one

of the predominant acids in wine grapes, combine with citric (found in oranges and lemons) and other active acids helping lower the pH value. The acid content of wine is one reason why Louis Pasteur called it "the most healthful and hygienic drink there is."

CHAPTER 2

WHAT IS WINE?

*A*T ITS SIMPLEST LEVEL, wine is a beverage resulting from the fermentation of the juice from grapes. Fermentation is a very complex chemical reaction whereby the sugar content of the grapes' juices is transformed by the action of yeast into approximately equal parts of carbon dioxide (CO_2) and alcohol. Both sugar and yeast naturally reside with the grape. As sugar is in the inside and yeast on the outside, fermentation is impossible to begin without crushing the grape or at least squeezing it enough to put the yeast in contact with the sugar. Since most wines are fermented in open top fermenters, the resultant carbon dioxide (CO_2) gas escapes into the air.

The yeast multiplies and continues to work until all the sugar is converted to alcohol and carbon dioxide unless the winemaker takes steps to preserve some of the sugar in the wine. This procedure is discussed in a later chapter. The alcohol, along with many other special attributes brought about by fermentation, remain in the wine. The final product, though, is more than alcohol, since fermentation brings out many flavors and aromas inherent in the grapes. As many as 300 different constituents in wine have been identified to date.

THE MAJOR TYPES OF WINE

For convenience in guiding the consumer as well as assessing and collecting federal taxes, wines have been divided into three broad categories: table wines, sparkling wines and dessert (or aperitif) wines.

Table wines are defined as those with an alcohol level of between 7% and 14% by volume. They are typically on the dry side ranging from under .1% residual sugar to 2.5%. Most experienced tasters cannot sense sugar at levels below .5% and cannot detect a change in the sugar level in increments of less than .5%. For example, you probably couldn't tell the difference in sugar levels between two wines if one were .7% residual sugar and the other 1%. But, you could probably tell which one was sweeter if one was .5% and the other 1%.

As the term implies, table wines are those which, over centuries, have been traditionally enjoyed with meals. On an average, table wines contain 12% alcohol and are basically dry. Table wines can be grouped into three classifications: varietal, generic and proprietary names.

Varietal wines are made predominantly from a single grape varietal, such as Cabernet Sauvignon or Chardonnay. By law (presently), a wine must contain at least 75% of wine from the grape varietal stated on the label. In practice, the content usually is on the order of 90% and often 100%.

Non-varietal wines are created by blending wines from several grape varietals into a harmonious whole. Wines labeled "Chablis," "Burgundy" and "Rosé" are generic

26

wines. Fortunately these terms, which refer to actual geographic locations such as "Chablis" (in France's Burgundy region), are being phased out and replaced with "White Table Wine" or "Red Table Wine." Using the names of French wine growing areas for domestic wines has the same effect on the French as it would on the Americans if the French labeled a wine "Napa Valley Red."

Proprietary wines are usually a blend of different grapes to attain a specific goal which could not be reached by using just one grape. The term "Meritage" was conceived for those wineries wishing to make wines from the "classic Bordeaux" varietals, namely Cabernet Sauvignon, Merlot, Cabernet Franc and occasionally Petite Verdot and Malbec for red, and Sauvignon Blanc and Semillon for white.

Sparkling wines are made by allowing a still wine to go through a second fermentation in a closed container. The container, whether a tank or a bottle, holds the carbon dioxide generated by the second fermentation in suspension, as opposed to letting it escape into the air, and that accounts for the bubbles.

"Champagne" is a sparkling wine made in the French region of Champagne using the French method of production referred to as "Methode Champenoise." "Spumante" is the Italian equivalent of Champagne, and in German "Sekt" means the same. Producers in the United States, South America and Australia often label their sparkling wines "Champagne," but European producers outside of the French Champagne region are not allowed to use the term by the European Economic Community (EEC) law. The three methods used in the creation of sparkling wines are: the charmat, or bulk process; the transfer process; and Methode Champenoise.

Methode Champenoise is considered the only true way to create sparkling wine. It is the only technique used to produce Champagne in France. However, other areas in France outside of Champagne make sparkling wine and they do not need to use the Champagne method. The finest sparkling wines produced in California and elsewhere are all created by this Champagne method. It is the most expensive of the three since it involves more labor. Each bottle may be handled 100 times or more.

To the surprise of many, Champagne is made primarily from red grapes. Champagne is normally pale white in color because the juice of the red grape is white. Red wines are made by allowing the white juice of the grape to come in contact with the red pigments in the skins for an extended period of time (7-14 days). If the grape is crushed quickly, only coming in contact with the skin for a few minutes, it will retain its white color.

As with any sparkling wine, the Champagne method starts with a still wine. The base wine, called the "cuvee," is usually a blend of several different vintages. This is done so that the winemaker can blend several different lots to make a cuvee that is consistent from one year to the next. This is more important in the Champagne region of France where the climate conditions are very unpredictable and only three or four years in ten produce the finest vintage Champagnes.

The grapes for Champagne are picked much earlier than grapes for table wine. At this stage in their development, there is very high acid, 1-1.5%, and very low sugar, 15-18%. These figures could not make a very good table wine as it would be too tart and acidic. The grapes are crushed until they are totally dry, leaving a wine which is tart, crisp and about 9-10% alcohol.

One of the most difficult jobs in winemaking is the blending of a Champagne cuvee. The master blender must take different lots of these very high acid, tart wines and imagine what they would taste like if they had bubbles. In some cases a blender could work with 100 different lots creating a cuvee using as little as 1% from a single lot.

Once the cuvee is decided upon, it is bottled in the traditional sparkling wine bottle to which a tiny amount of sugar solution and yeast is added and the bottle sealed with a crown cap. Fermentation takes place all over again (referred to as the second fermentation) and the sparkling wine is born.

As the yeast converts the sugar to alcohol (this raises the total alcohol level to the desired 12% level), the other byproduct, carbon dioxide, has no place to go but back into the wine, thus making those wonderful little bubbles which separates Champagne from all other wines. The yeast cells die off and fall to the bottom.

The difference between the three methods lies in the aging and clarification technique since, with the Methode Champenoise, the sparkling wine never leaves the bottle it was created in. Once each day, the cellarman gives each bottle a slight shake and quarter turn. This is called riddling and the rack it is done on is called a riddling rack. With each turn the bottle is reinserted at a new, more upright angle until it is perfectly vertical, cork side down.

After about two to six months of this treatment, all of the sediment (expired yeast cells) is collected at the neck of the bottle and the yeast, having done their best, have retired to yeast heaven. The bottles are placed in special racks for aging on the expired yeast cells for as many as one to five years. The longer they rest on the yeast, the more complex the flavors become. The wine can actually pick up a "yeasty" component reminiscent of fresh baked bread.

While the sparkling wine is now basically complete one problem remains. The expired yeast cells would form an unsightly, cloudy haze if the bottle were turned upright. They must be removed without disturbing the delicate sparkling wine which they helped create. To accomplish this task, the bottles are carefully removed from the racks and placed neck down in a solution, usually liquid nitrogen. The bottleneck and approximately the first two inches of wine are frozen. The crown cap is removed and the CO_2 pressure within the bottle (approximately 70 lbs. per sq. in.) forces out the two inch ice "plug" containing the sediment. This is how the wine is clarified of the sediment (expired yeast cells). The bottle is then filled with either the same sparkling wine for a Natural (very dry) wine or it is topped off with a touch of sugar and wine for Brut (dry) or Extra Dry; (slightly less dry) versions. It then receives its traditional cork, wire hood and foil, and may be sold or held for additional aging. Sparkling wine made by the Methode Champenoise technique can be identified by the legend "Made in This Bottle."

This technique was perfected in the early 1800s by the Madam Clicquot of the famous Champagne house which bares her name, Veuve Clicquot. That name literally translates as "The Widow Clicquot." She was left a widow in her twenties and inherited the winery her husband had founded. After perfecting this technique (called disgorgement) she went on a sales trip to Russia and became the most successful Champagne house in France. To this day, Russia is still one of the largest markets for Champagne in the world.

The terms Natural, Brut, and Extra Dry, carry no legal

definition. For instance, it is generally accepted that a Brut has between .75% and 1.5% residual sugar and an Extra Dry between 1.2% and 2%. That would mean that one producer's Extra Dry could technically be drier than another's Brut. This much sugar in a table wine would taste sweet to most people. However, because the grapes used for sparkling wine are picked at lower sugar and much higher acid (and the bubbles actually hide some of the sweet taste because not all of the liquid is attacking your taste buds at the same time), the perception of sweetness is not as apparent. While many sparkling wine drinkers prefer dry wines, most would find a Natural "too dry" as the acid is fairly penetrating.

With the transfer process the cuvee, together with a tiny amount of the sugar and yeast solution, is stored in a large container, usually glass, so it can be said to be made in the bottle. The secondary fermentation takes place within this large bottle which is usually much larger than the one in which it will be sold, sometimes 10-20 times larger. The resulting sparkling wine is then aged in the bottle for a period of six months to a year. Since the secondary fermentation produces "sediment," mainly spent yeast cells, the sediment must be removed. The cap is removed and the bottle contents poured into a vat. This must be done in a pressure controlled environment or the bubbles will dissipate faster than you can say "pop."

The sparkling wine is then filtered and rebottled in a new bottle under high pressure conditions to insure minimum loss of CO_2. The transfer process is more expensive than charmat because of its longer aging time "on the yeast," and the hand work involved. It is less expensive than Methode Champenoise because of the method used to filter the yeast cells. Modern methods for Methode Champenoise production, which include the gyroplate for riddling an entire pallet (48 cases) at a time, makes the transfer method almost all but obsolete. Transfer process sparkling wine is identified by the term "Made in The Bottle." Ideally it was the gap between the expensive, but tasty, Methode Champenoise and the inexpensive, but bland, charmat.

With the charmat process, the base wine, or cuvee, is placed in a sealed, pressure-resistant tank and injected with a small amount of sugar solution and yeast. The yeast attacks the sugar causing a second fermentation which generates CO_2 gas. Since this gas cannot escape the tank, it is absorbed by the wine and forms bubbles. The finished sparkling wine is then filtered for clarity and bottled. Sparkling wine produced by this process is the least expensive because it requires no hand work, can be produced rapidly, and spends very little time in contact with the yeast. This is an important point because the wine's extended contact with the spent yeast cells is what gives sparkling wine its unique flavor.

Besides the method of production, the grapes, or cuvee, are also very important. The best grapes for making Champagne and sparkling wine are Pinot Noir, Pinot Munier (mostly used in France) and Chardonnay. Most producers will not go through the trouble and expense of making wine in the traditional Methode Champenoise way and use inexpensive grapes. Conversely, charmat producers don't need expensive Chardonnay and Pinot Noir grapes for what will eventually be a very inexpensive wine. The government makes no distinction, however, imposing the stiffest tax on sparkling wine over any other type;

almost $1.00 per bottle regardless of whether it is the finest vintage Champagne, or the lowest charmat bulk product.

Aperitif and dessert; wines, although enjoyed on different occasions, are two groups usually lumped together because of their legal definitions based on alcohol content. In the making of what we call fortified wines such as Port, the fermentation process is arrested before completion with the addition of a neutral spirit such as grape alcohol. As the yeast is converting the sugar to alcohol, the addition of spirits raises the alcohol level to 20%. Since yeast cannot live in an alcohol environment of more than 17%, this procedure will effectively kill off all the yeast cells. Because they have not finished converting all the sugar to alcohol and CO_2, whatever residual sugar is left before the addition of the spirits will now be in the finished wine. In the case of Port the residual sugar could be as low as 8% or as high as 12% depending on the desire of the winemaker.

The Federal Government defines any wine that has been fortified with alcohol by the addition of brandy or neutral spirits as a liqueur. The taxes paid on these products are almost three times that of table wines. Their alcohol level ranges from 14% to 21%. It is possible (indeed, it is done often) for a table wine to reach a natural alcohol level of as much as 17%. Once the wine crosses the 14% border it must pay the extra tax regardless of whether it reached that level naturally or not. This tax accounts for the large number of table wines labeled 13.9% alcohol.

The most popular wines in the aperitif and dessert category are Sherry and Port. Port, a red wine quite sweet to the taste, takes its name from Portugal where it first was created. Port-styled wine is made by many countries including South Africa, Australia and California. Port nearly always is a blend of several grape varietals. Its high level of sweetness make it ideal with desserts, or as a nightcap. Sherry is an amber-colored wine which originated in the Spanish town of Jerez. The English, the biggest importers of Sherry in the world, couldn't pronounce Jerez (Hare-eth) so they called it "Jare-ezz" and finally Sherry. It ranges from very dry to very sweet. The driest and lightest colored Sherry is called "Fino." Amontillado is a Sherry of medium amber hue, and usually somewhat sweeter than Fino. California Sherries labeled simply "Sherry" fall somewhat into this category but do not compare directly with the Spanish version. The heaviest and most full-bodied Sherry produced in Spain is "oloroso." It is usually rather dark in color and can be either dry or sweet. The Fino and Amontillado types are aperitif wines, while the oloroso is either a food or dessert wine.

OTHER TYPES OF WINE

The large and luscious late harvest wines are produced from grapes which have been left on the vine longer than those destined to become table wines. They develop a naturally higher than normal sugar level, thus the resulting wine may be higher in alcohol, often over 14%. More often, however, they are higher in sugar since the fermentation process is arrested before all the sugar is converted. This is done by either putting the wine through a filter fine enough to remove the yeast or lowering the temperature of the wine to almost freezing (34°). This causes the yeast to stop working and fall to the bottom of the tank where it can be removed easily.

Late harvest Zinfandels were popular in the late 1960s and early 1970s, but have almost disappeared due to lack of consumer interest and competition from Port.

White wines in the late harvest style are generally made from the Riesling grape, as is traditional in Germany where they first evolved. In France, a similar style of wine is called "Sauternes." This wine is made from a blend of Sauvignon Blanc and Semillon.

Late harvest Rieslings are made in several different sweetness levels similar in style to those found in Germany where they are labeled as Spätlese (late picked), Auslese (very late picked), Beerenauslese (individually picked ripe clusters) and Trockenbeerenauslese (individually picked ripe grapes). In California, these terms are illegal to use; therefore, late harvest is generally the only term applied to the wines in this style.

One of the key terms in late harvest wines is "Botrytis." It refers to a special, beneficial mold called Botrytis cinerea. This mold causes the grapes to shrivel and dehydrate, while at the same time concentrating their natural flavors and sugars. The result is a rather rare wine, very sweet, with the flavor of honey and apricots. They are very difficult and very costly to produce and, as a result, very expensive. For example, an acre vineyard planted with Chardonnay would yield about 200 to 250 cases of fine table wine. That same vineyard may only yield 50 cases of a late harvest wine.

CHAPTER 3

TYPES AND LABELING OF WINE

*T*HERE ARE BASICALLY THREE WAYS to label a bottle of wine: 1) by region, 2) by varietal, 3) make something up. Regional labeling is widely practiced in Europe, varietal labeling is widespread in the United States and the New World. Everybody makes up names for wines that don't fit into either category.

Regional names can range from a country (Product of Italy) to a tiny plot of land such as Pauillac in the Bordeaux region of France. In Italy, a wine may be named Chianti, a large region, or Barolo, a smaller one. It could also take its name from a single, small vineyard within Chianti or Barolo. The use of place names on wine labels in the major European districts is carefully regulated by each country's government. The most obvious examples are the French AOC (Appellation d'Origine Contrôlée) and the Italian DOC (Denominazione di Origine Controllata); both translate to "The wine in this bottle comes from a controlled place of origin and must conform to certain laws regarding grape production, yields and processing." The Italians have added another tier, DOCG, with the "G" standing for "Guarantita," and comes with a guarantee of quality, having been approved by a revue board that actually tastes the wine.

In varietal labeling the wine is named after the predominant grape used. Each country has its own specific laws regarding what percentage of the named grape on the label must be in the bottle. For instance, an American wine labeled "Chardonnay" must contain at least 75% of Chardonnay grapes in it. In certain parts of France where wines are labeled with the grape name, such as in Alsace and occasionally Burgundy, it must be made from 100% of the stated varietal.

Fortunately the use of European place names Chablis, Burgundy, Champagne, Chianti, Rhine and others, on wines made outside of those regions, is now a rarity in California. It was common practice in the 1970s and into the 1980s. These names refer to proper, geographic areas. Inherent in the names are the grapes used to make the wine. All white Burgundy is made from Chardonnay grapes; all red Burgundy from Pinot Noir grapes. It's the law! The same goes for wines from Barolo and Barbaresco which must be made from Nebbiolo grapes.

Wineries in the United States and in other non-European countries freely use these place names for their generic wines. In most instances they are offering wines made from a potpourri of grapes that are similar only in color to the European originals. A "California Rhine" or "Australian Rhine" is just a white wine, usually the least expensive. The EEC has agreed not to use the proper names of these geographic locals in the labeling of wines not from these regions. You won't find European wines labeled Chianti or Chablis unless they come from Chianti or Chablis.

Below is a listing of the most common varietals world wide and a brief description of their flavor characteristics.

- **CHARDONNAY:** One of two "noble" white grapes grown. A medium to full-bodied white wine that often suggests hints of green apples, pears and, sometimes, spice. Known to be one of the most complex, long-lived dry white wines made. In Burgundy, France, Chardonnay reaches its pinnacle of perfection along with its pinnacle of price. While many California, Italian and Australian wine-makers use Burgundy as their model, few have been able to attain the components in their wines that send wine connoisseurs into rhapsodic ramblings. Should be served cool, but not too cold.

- **RIESLING:** Occasionally labeled "Johannisberg Riesling." This misnomer stems from the use of the township where one of the finest Rieslings in the world is grown, Johannisberg, Germany, in the Rheingau. The most typical versions smell like fresh cut flowers, apples and apricot blossoms. Many are made in a slightly sweet style. Like Chardonnay, it is the other noble white grape and can age for many years. Should be served cool, but not too cold.

- **CHENIN BLANC:** A lighter-styled white wine often reminiscent of ripe melons and peaches; occasionally has a slightly herbal aroma. In California this wine can be very dry or very sweet. Most fall in the middle. In Vouvray, France, it takes on totally different flavor profiles of pineapple and spice, along with a gripping acidity, and can be aged for many years. Should be served slightly chilled.

- **SAUVIGNON BLANC** or **FUMÉ BLANC:** Medium-bodied with a distinctive fresh grassy aroma, sometimes peppery, and also reminiscent of gunflint in character. Fumé Blanc means "white smoke" in French and many describe this wine as "smoky" in character. It is a white wine to be enjoyed when young or after a few years of aging and is normally very dry. Should be served cool, but not too cold.

• GEWÜRZTRAMINER: Often, in California, a slightly sweet white wine with a unique spicy, musk-oil scent that is assertive. From Alsace, France, and the upper regions of Italy near Tyrol, it can take on more powerful components, age for many years and is normally very dry. Should be served slightly chilled.

• CABERNET SAUVIGNON: One of two "noble" red varieties. More often than not deep, garnet red in color, often with an herbaceous and green-olive aroma and flavor, tannic (astringent) in taste and dry. While California's warm climate ripens Cabernet with very consistent results, Bordeaux's marginal climate forces it to be planted in the Medoc region, near the more temperate Atlantic coast. Cabernet can be aged for many years and often benefits greatly from it. Should be served at room temperature (approximately 60°).

• PINOT NOIR: The other noble red grape. A medium-bodied dry red wine with an aroma ranging from peppermint and spice to cherry, rose petals, violets and truffles. It is enjoyed for its smooth, silky texture and transforms with bottle age into one of the greatest wines produced on earth. It is one of the most difficult grapes to grow and most difficult wines to make. Lukewarm public acceptance, except for the top Burgundies from France, keep its price below Cabernet. Since the early '90s, however, dramatic improvements in quality from California's top producers as well as a strong interest in lighter, more approachable wines to go with lighter foods has seen this grape gain a considerable foothold in the red wine arena. Should be served at room temperature (approximately 60°).

• **GAMAY:** A lighter-bodied red wine similar to Pinot Noir in flavor, but with more accented fruit and an aroma like that of raspberries and strawberries. Gamay reaches its pinnacle in the Beaujolais region of France. Should be served at slightly below room temperature (approximately 55°).

• **MERLOT:** A distinct, dry, medium to full-bodied red wine with an aroma similar to plums and cherries with hints of black tea, chocolate and coffee. Its gentle fruit components are often used to soften Cabernet's hard edge. It ripens earlier than Cabernet,making it, along with its softer character and different fruit flavors, a perfect addition in the Bordeaux region. Besides being a flavor enhancer, it also provides an insurance policy against inclement weather destroying the Cabernet crop. In those cases, the wine would have more Merlot in it. In California, it is often used to blend with Cabernet as well as standing on its own, occasionally with Cabernet blended in for added body. Should be served at room temperature (approximately 60°).

• **PETITE SIRAH:** A rather rough, full-bodied red wine with a berry-like aroma and flavor, usually quite tannic (puckery in the mouth) and deep in color; the best are reminiscent of black pepper in aroma and flavor. Was mislabeled because it was thought to be a direct descendent of the powerful Syrah grape of the northern Rhone. It has since been discovered that it's not even a distant cousin, but the name has stuck. Should be served at room temperature (approximately 60°).

• **Zinfandel:** A California original in that its origin is not known for sure. An all-purpose red wine that is produced in a wide variety of styles. The typical aspect of the varietal is a berry-like character, similar to raspberries or strawberries. Generally fruity, somewhat spicy in nature. Should be served at room temperature (approximately 60°).

• OTHER VARIETALS: Most other varietals are not as easy to recognize because they have not been as exposed to the general wine drinking public. They are no less exciting and in many cases can be more appreciated by consumers because of their differences. Among the white wines offered as varietals, the following are popular, but can best be described as fruity in nature, and "vinous," meaning wine-like: FRENCH COLOMBARD, light with gracious flavors of melon and pear; MARSANNE, spicy and minerally; VIOGNIER, very spicy and extracted; PINOT BLANC, slight banana and peach flavors; and SEMILLON, fig and herbal scents. Among the red wines in this mold are several popular wines: BARBERA, spicy, but can be astringent; CARIGNAN, soft berry fruit; CABERNET FRANC, cranberry and spice; GRENACHE, minerally and spicy; and SYRAH, peppery and black cherry.

CHAPTER 4

COMPARING WINES

*W*INES PRODUCED in California and Europe are often from the same grapes and are too often directly compared. While there may be similarities with regard to the varieties used, the soil and climate are often so different (not to mention the skill, experience and style objectives of the winemakers) that these comparisons can be the truest form of the "apples versus oranges" cliché. This is not to say we shouldn't plant or make Pinot Noir because it won't taste like Burgundy, or Nebbiolo because it won't taste like Barbaresco. I believe a winemaker's first duty is to make a wine which is true to the grape and vineyard. France makes the best French wine in the world. Oregon makes the best Oregon wine in the world. While you should revere great wines and try to emulate their greatness, I don't believe we should be trying to copy them. These lofty goals usually end in failure. We should try to do our best with what we have to work with instead of making a "me too" wine.

The following is a listing of premium grapes and their

origin or best known areas of production.

UNITED STATES	OTHER COUNTRIES

REDS

Cabernet Sauvignon	Bordeaux, France; Chile; Australia
Merlot	Bordeaux, France; Friulis, Chile; Italy
Pinot Noir	Burgundy, France
Syrah/Mourvedre/Grenache	Rhone and Provence, France; Australia
Sangiovese	Chianti, Italy
Nebbiolo	Piedmont (Barolo, Barbaresco), Italy
Barbera	Piedmont, Italy

WHITES

Chenin Blanc	Vouvray, France; South Africa; Australia
Chardonnay	Burgundy and Chablis, France; South Africa; Chile; Australia
Sauvignon Blanc (Fume Blanc)	Sancerre and Pouilly Fume, France; South Africa; Chile; Australia
Sauvignon Blanc/Semillon	Graves, France
Riesling	Alsace, France; Mosel, Rheingau,Germany; South Africa; Australia
Gewurztraminer	Alsace, France; Rhinehessen, Germany; Friuli, Italy

VINTAGE DATES

The vintage date tells when the grapes were picked and converted into wine. It says nothing about when the wine was placed in the bottle or when it became available to the consumer.

This date can provide useful information because it is often the only gauge of quality we have to go on. Vintage conditions vary from year to year. Mother Nature is unpredictable, often bringing hailstorms, frost, rains, unusual cold or hot spells at the wrong time. Wide vintage variation and, occasionally, total losses, are a way of life for the winegrowers of Europe. The big difference in California and many other temperate areas is that the wine crop seldom experiences a major loss or a vintage of very poor quality.

For most of the world's finest wines, knowing about a specific vintage is helpful because it tells you something about the wine's quality and also about its aging potential.

CALIFORNIA HISTORY

European grapes were first brought to California in the mid-nineteenth century by several pioneers. The main source of grapes from Europe came from one man, Count Augustine Haraszthy. He somehow convinced the governor of California in the 1850s to finance a trip to Europe to bring back cuttings from the finest vineyards and help begin a wine industry here.

California wines enjoyed a short spurt of success until a vine pest called phylloxera, which attacks the root system of vines, destroyed many of the vineyards. The curiosity of European winemakers is what brought American rootstock, along with phylloxera, to Europe. The phylloxera pest lives benignly in American rootstock without doing much damage. Once, however, it was introduced to those succulent vines from Europe, it feasted on every vine it could find until there were no more vines to destroy. By the end of the nineteenth century, there was hardly a vine standing in all of Europe.

The cure for this worldwide blight brought California and European winemakers close together. Native American vines, called *Vitis Labrusca*, were resistant to phylloxera, but produced wine of lesser quality than European *Vitis Vinifera* vines. Europe was slow to realize this cure or it would have recovered from phylloxera in less than five years. As it was, it took almost 50 years for the devastation to be controlled. Today, nearly all of the world's vines are a composite of American rootstock and European vine stock.

As Europe was ridding itself of phylloxera, California was struck by Prohibition. Prohibition extended from 1920 to 1933, virtually destroying the wine industry except for a few wineries which made wines for "medicinal" or "sacramental" purposes. Apparently, along with Prohibition came a newfound interest in religion because there was probably never so much sacramental wines made than during this period.

After the repeal of Prohibition, California began the slow process of rebuilding its wine industry. Since most of the fine wine grapes had been pulled out to plant more "legal" crops, the wineries were forced to begin an industry just like they had 70 years earlier. They concentrated on quantity instead of quality as a way to jump-start the industry. Inexpensive "jug" wines and sweet dessert wines were the order of the day. They lived on the philosophy that less money and more wine was the only way to go. For years very little fine wine came out of California. Most was sold in jugs and in carloads to be bottled elsewhere under anonymous names. The revival of California fine wines did not occur until the early 1960s when, with increased demand for table wines, vineyards of noble varietals were reestablished.

Europe's wine history in both viticulture and winemaking goes back centuries, while California's industry basically began in the 1950s and 1960s, other states even later. Progress has been rapid thanks to highly innovative scientific practices unencumbered by tradition. Extensive microbiological research and fermentation techniques that were developed in California are responsible for the delicate, finely flavored white wines we have today. Yet, in keeping with tradition, California, Washington, Oregon and other state's winemakers still age their wines in small oak barrels while fermentation is carried out in the most modern temperature-controlled stainless steel tanks or hygienically sound barrels. Vineyards, too, have moved forward with stricter crop control, organic farming and pest control. Modern methods for growing grapes also have made dramatic improvements in quality. California's wine production is a combination of Old World traditions and New World technology.

EVOLUTION OF CALIFORNIA WINE

California began a massive vineyard expansion in the 1960s that helped double the existing acreage in one decade. The current total acreage is 333,000. The number of wineries increased from 245 in 1970 to well over 800 (and still counting) by 1996. The wines have improved to the point that America competes on a quality level with the world's finest offerings. This does not mean that we should make direct comparisons of one wine against another. Two wines could be of equal quality but taste completely different.

The vineyard expansion is an important part of the success story. For the most part, the new vineyards were planted with varieties of higher quality and in locales better suited to their needs. When Haraszthy returned from his famous voyage a hundred years earlier, he sold off more than 100,000 cuttings of European grape varieties. Unfortunately, he was a better salesman than a viticulturist. Vines were sold without regard for where they should be planted. Cool climate grapes went to hot climates and vice versa. After a hundred years of experiments and Prohibition, winemakers began to see the light.

A greater availability of higher quality wine grapes began to emerge in the early 1970s. Zinfandel became the most widely planted red wine grape. Cabernet Sauvignon went from nonexistence to third in a few short years. For white wines, enormous new plantings were made of Chardonnay and Chenin Blanc. Plantings of Sauvignon Blanc were doubled.

New wineries with new winemakers and new ideas had much to do with the improvement in quality. Most are small specialists, dedicated to producing handcrafted wines. They helped create a spirit of intense, but usually friendly, competition. Many came into the business with a solid understanding of the economics and the capital-intensive nature of winemaking. Many of these wineries were owned by families that had been very successful in other businesses. Small wineries began mixing high technology and state-of-the-art equipment with traditional approaches, combining the best of both worlds.

This is not to say that the wine industry doesn't have its share of people who don't have the foggiest notion about what they are doing. The wine business is as romantic and exciting an endeavor as one could imagine being involved in. Many are attracted by the romance and "lifestyle." As we shall see later, it is a very difficult and unpredictable business which, like any other, requires brains, brawn and marketing savvy to stay afloat.

CHAPTER 5

THE WORLD'S WINE REGIONS

*T*HE HISTORY OF ANY WINE REGION is what makes it unique. Some go along making perfectly ordinary wines from a given grape because they've been doing it that way for centuries. A different grape planted in the same vineyard could yield a much finer wine. World demand and competition probably won't allow this situation to continue for too long except possibly on a very small, individual scale.

The following is a list of the major grape growing regions and sub-regions which have earned an important position in the market and have a history of making superior wines. Many other areas are becoming known and, when this book is re-written in 10 years, they may be more famous than the following.

CALIFORNIA'S WINE REGIONS

• SIERRA FOOTHILLS: Located in the Sierra Foothills this name is known for big, buxom Zinfandels. The style is very ripe, full-bodied, often quite tannic (astringent). Classic Chenin Blancs are also produced.

- ALEXANDER VALLEY: A large section of Sonoma County. To date it is a proven area for Chardonnay, Cabernet Sauvignon and Zinfandel, and more recently, Merlot.
- CARNEROS: A vineyard section at the southern tips of the Napa and Sonoma County line. It has an especially cool climate that has been specifically suited for Pinot Noir, Chardonnay and, occasionally, Merlot.
- CENTRAL VALLEY: The largest vineyard area in California. It is responsible for most of the state's generic table wines and, more recently, showing promise with the better varietals, specifically Zinfandel and Cabernet Sauvignon.
- DRY CREEK: A subregion in northern Sonoma best known for producing some of the best Zinfandels in the state as well as superb Sauvignon Blanc and Cabernet Sauvignon.
- EDNA VALLEY: The first area in the Central Coast to be singled out for producing quality wines, specifically Chardonnay, in the mid-1970s and still going strong.
- LIVERMORE: One of the oldest grape growing districts, it is best known for Sauvignon Blanc and Semillon, along with excellent Petite Sirah and Cabernet Sauvignon.
- MENDOCINO: This region is really two separate areas. Anderson Valley, near the coast, is known for exceptional Chardonnay and Pinot Noir as well as sparkling wine made from the same grapes. Further inland is the area around Ukiah which is much warmer. This region produces excellent red wines such as Zinfandel, Cabernet Sauvignon, Petite Sirah and, occasionally, good Chardonnay and Pinot Noir.
- MONTEREY: One of the state's coolest wine districts. So far the best wines are Riesling, Pinot Noir and Chardonnay, although Cabernet has accounted for some

striking examples in the warmer microclimates.

- NAPA VALLEY: The most famous and most established wine district. It is consistently successful with Cabernet Sauvignon and Sauvignon Blanc, ranking among the state's best. Zinfandel and Riesling have their pockets and Chardonnay has been successful on the hillsides.

- RUSSIAN RIVER: A very cool region in Northern Sonoma producing many of the best Pinot Noirs in the state as well as classy and stylistic Chardonnays.

- SAN LUIS OBISPO: A new region showing fine promise for Cabernet Sauvignon, Zinfandel and Sauvignon Blanc. Pinot Noir has been inconsistent in quality as have other varietals that do well in cool climates, specifically Chardonnay.

- SANTA BARBARA: A relatively new region, showing excellent results with Gewürztraminer, Riesling and Sauvignon Blanc. It is becoming best known for striking Chardonnays and Pinot Noirs. Cabernet Franc and Merlot, especially when blended with careful lots of Cabernet Sauvignon, are superb. A few wineries have crafted some excellent examples of Bordeaux-style wines made from these grapes.

- SONOMA: Much larger than Napa, and just as well established, it is only now receiving national recognition. Zinfandel and Petite Sirah are strong points, but the Chardonnays and Cabernet Sauvignons are the highlights.

- Other Areas: In 1970 there were a handful of viticultural areas. These areas were defined by the government to be significantly different both in geography and geology to claim a place on the label. All wines from Napa Valley were labeled Napa Valley as long as 95% of the grapes came from there. The same for Sonoma County, Mendocino

County, etc. Since then we have seen a proliferation of more than 300 areas being identified and allowed to adorn the label. So, if you have a good memory, you'll know that Howell Mountain is in Napa County, Sierra Madre is in Santa Barbara County and Anderson Valley is in Mendocino County because the labels don't have to tell you.

• **Other States:** It's hard to believe that in 1980, nearly 97% of all the wine made in the United States was made in California. Today, it is less than 90% and dropping. While we have known of the fine wine growing areas of the Willamette Valley in Oregon, the Finger Lakes in New York and the Yakima Valley of Washington, the production was too small to be a challenge. Now, combined with Idaho, Texas and more than 30 other states with bonded wineries, many bold winemakers are learning to deal with the elements which prevented them from making world-class wine. It's just a matter of time.

FRANCE'S WINE REGIONS

France is the most famous wine producing country in the world. Many of its wines are the models which other winemakers try to emulate. The climates in most of its areas, especially in the north, are cold and damp, making complete ripening of the grapes quite difficult in two to four vintages out of ten. France allows the addition of sugar during fermentation when the vintage is poor and the grapes never attain enough sugar naturally to make an acceptable wine. More than a few winemakers, however, add sugar (called chaptalization) as a matter of course and without regard for the vintage.

• ALSACE: *Located in the northeast corner of France,*

along the German border, Alsace specializes in white wines. These wines are much drier than those made in Germany. The finest of the lot is Gewürztraminer-dry, spicy and forceful; and Riesling-dry, minerally and perfect with the cuisine of the region. Other wines of note include a light, crisp Sylvaner, and Pinot Blanc and Pinot Gris. The wines vary with the vintage, but not as radically as the wines of Germany.

• BEAUJOLAIS: *A large area at the southern tip of Burgundy which produces the fresh, fruity and lively red wine for every-day pleasure.* Made from the Gamay grape, Beaujolais is fermented to emphasize fruit over structure. The aroma is similar to strawberry jam and, though deep in color, the wine is soft on the palate. Wines labeled "Beaujolais-Villages" come from two or more villages which produce more substantial wines than the "Beaujolais" offerings. Finer by far are the ten "Crus" of Beaujolais produced from grapes grown in one specific village. The ten villages are: Saint-Amour, Julienas, Chenas, Moulin-a-Vent, Fleurie, Chiroubles, Morgon, Brouilly, Regnie and Côtes de Brouilly. A small amount of Beaujolais Blanc (White Beaujolais made from Chardonnay) is exported to the United States. The best are fruity and crisp, but not very distinctive. Nouveau wine is the first of the Beaujolais to be released. It is sold, by law, no sooner than the third Thursday in November, barely two months after it is picked. Nouveau is typically light and fruity and should be consumed within four months of release.

• BORDEAUX: *The most famous wine region in France,* Bordeaux is known for wines which are a blend of Merlot, Cabernet Sauvignon, Malbec, Petite Verdot and Cabernet Franc. The wines from here are among the best known, most expensive and long-lived wines in the world. However, Bordeaux is the single largest wine producing area on earth. Most of Bordeaux wines are fairly ordinary. It is mainly the wines from the areas in the center of Bordeaux, like the Medoc and Graves and the eastern bank in St. Emilion and Pomerol where the best wines are made. In great vintages, wines from these areas possess all the fine qualities and sturdy structure of the greatest wines imaginable. Within the Medoc area are small villages, most notably Pauillac, St. Estephe and St. Julian where the top chateaux are found. White Bordeaux, primarily made from Sauvignon Blanc and Semillon, has taken its place of greatness along with the reds with regard to their deep, complex flavors, ageability and price.

• BURGUNDY: In this area, the red wines are made from Pinot Noir, and vary in quality from light and ordinary to rich, complex and majestic. Generally, the smaller the area, the better the wine. Burgundy's finest wines come from the Côte d'Or, a mere 30 mile strip divided at the center into two distinct parts; the Côte de Nuits in the north and the Côte de Beaune in the south. The Nuits produces 95% red wines from the Pinot Noir grape. These are among the finest, longest-lived and most exotic and expensive wines made on earth.

The Côte de Beaune produces approximately 38% white wine, 60% red and 2% sparkling. White Burgundy is made exclusively from Chardonnay. Quality varies from the finest, Montrachets and Corton Charlemagnes, to a simple Macon Blanc. The best ones from the villages of Meursault, Puligny and Chassagne are aged in small oak barrels. Wines from the Macon are generally non-oak aged and offer good quality, on the order of Pouilly-Fuissé, but for less money. The reds of Beaune are not as revered as the reds of the Côte de Nuits. They are normally lighter in style; however, they can produce wines in good vintages that rival Côte de Nuits and beyond.

• CHABLIS: This region is part of Burgundy although it is not connected directly. Wines are made almost exclusively from the Chardonnay grape in a dry, crisp style with shy fruit and a flinty character due to the high chalk content of the soil. Seldom aged in small oak barrels although a few renegades are conducting some successful experiments.

• CHAMPAGNE: This area is believed to create the finest sparkling wine of all. The best offer excellent, tiny bubbles (a sign of quality) and a yeasty aroma with fruity, complex flavors. The most common grape here is the Pinot Meunier, a red grape, along with Pinot Noir and Chardonnay.

• LOIRE VALLEY: A long, diverse region in western France adjacent to the Loire River that produces wines from charming and fruity to rich and long-lived and even a few exceptional Rosés. The whites are predominantly from the Chenin Blanc (Vouvray), Melon de Bourgogne (Muscadet) and Sauvignon Blanc (Sancerre, Pouilly Fumé) varietals. The reds are made from Cabernet Franc and occasionally Cabernet Sauvignon and Pinot Noir.

• RHONE VALLEY: A long, narrow strip in the southern center of France about 60 miles long and not more than five miles wide. It is cut in two by the soil and climate changes making the Rhone almost two regions in one. The northern section is best known for fabled and long-lived red wines: Hermitage, Côte Rôtie, St. Joseph and Cornas and a fragrant white, Condrieu from the Viognier grape. The south is famous for the full-bodied Chateauneuf-du-Pape and Gigondas and the light Rosés from Tavel. Hermitage and Côte Rôtie are made from the hearty, intense Syrah grape with a tiny bit of white wine added to soften it. Chateauneuf-du-Pape can be a blend of up to thirteen different varieties, three of them white. Gigondas uses the same red grapes as Chateauneuf-du-Pape but no white. Most are a blend of the major grapes of the area; Grenache, Mourvedre, Syrah and Cinsault. Wines labeled Côtes du Rhone come from the south and are a blend of five to ten different varieties from the region. In recent years, many Côtes du Rhone reds are being discovered by Americans for both flavor and value. Very little white Rhone wine is made.

ITALY'S WINES

Italy is the largest wine producing area in the world, producing nearly one billion cases annually. As recently as 1970, a very large portion was used for distilling as it was not good enough to be made into table wine. Another large portion was used to blend with other countries' wines, especially France's, to help strengthen their wines in weaker vintages.

While the DOC laws established in 1963 and the DOCG laws of 1980 are a bold step in controlling quality, only 25% of all Italian wines fall into these categories. The term "Classico" refers to the center of the area. Chianti Classico, for example, is in the center of Chianti and is usually a better wine than most from outside the "Classico" area simply labeled "Chianti."

• BAROLO: In the state of Piedmont, one of the richest, most complex of Italian red wines. Made from the Nebbiolo grape, the wine has incredible depth and extraordinary aging potential. Similar, but on a lesser scale, are wines labeled Nebbiolo, Spanna and Gattinara.

• BARBARESCO: Also a Piedmont wine made from Nebbiolo, but from an area a few miles southwest of Barolo. It's normally very rich and concentrated, but generally not as tannic as Barolo.

• BARBERA: The most prolific red grape in all of Italy. It produces as simple a wine as can be imagined, or a very complex, oak-aged, low yield wine of intensity and character. It can exhibit robust black cherry and spicy, leathery flavors.

• BRUNELLO DI MONTALCINO: A relatively new wine made from the Brunello grape grown in the town of Montalcino a few miles east of Chianti in Tuscany. This grape is an isolated clone of the Sangiovese grown in Chianti. It produces a much heartier, tannic and longer-lived wine than the Sangiovese grown in Chianti. It was cultivated in the late 1800s and is now one of the most popular of Italy's hearty reds.

• Chianti: Is in the state of Tuscany and is made from several grape varieties, predominantly Sangiovese. Chianti is a red wine with strong aroma, medium-body and a slight sharpness in flavor. Chianti Classico comes from a smaller and normally finer area, and offers more depth, flavor and complexity. The "Riserva" wines can live for many years. By law, Classico must be aged for one year in the barrel, Reservas for two. Non-Classico Chiantis of note come from Rufina, Colli, Senesi and Siena.

• FRASCATI: A fresh, light, lively white wine made in Latium. It's best enjoyed for its soft, fruity appeal.

• ORVIETO: A white wine growing in popularity from the state of Umbria. Made from the Trebbiano grape, it is fruity, smooth and flavorful. The "Classico" versions are richer and more age-worthy.

- PINOT GRIGIO: One of Italy's most popular white wines. Made from the grape of the same name, the wine is usually light and delicate with a peach, pear and apple fruit flavor. The best come from the Northern areas of Veneto, Friuli and Trentino.

- SOAVE: A clean, modestly fragrant, white wine, occasionally retaining some sweetness for added interest. It's Made in the Veneto.

- VALPOLICELLA: A popular Venetian light-bodied red, with simple aromas and a slightly rough flavor. Enjoyable with food.

- VINO DA TAVOLA: The lowest quality designation. Any grape or combination of grapes could be used and it is not normally thought of as a quality product.

GERMANY'S WINE REGIONS

Germany has one of the coldest, shortest growing seasons of all major wine regions. Consequently, only a few grape varieties, and only in good vintages, are capable of becoming ripe enough to turn into wine. Like France, Germany allows the addition of sugar during fermentation when the vintage is poor and the grapes never attain enough sugar naturally to make an acceptable wine.

The two major growing regions are the Rhine Valley and the Mosel. The finer wines in each come from vineyards adjacent to their respective rivers (the Rhine and the Mosel) which provide a more temperate climate. Germany is famous for its Riesling, but the predominant grape planted here is a crossbreed, Müller-Thurgau. If the varietal is stated on the label it must be 100%, if not so stated it can be anything.

Germany's most famous and sought-after wines have a touch of sugar in them. This is normally balanced by a gripping acidity which often masks the presence of the sugar. There is a current move in Germany to make more dry white wines, since the country is identified as a sweet wine producer. "Trocken" (dry) or "halbtrocken" (half-dry) are the key words indicating the wine's dryness.

The system of labeling wines in Germany is based upon the condition or ripeness of the grapes at the time of harvest. Too often, Germany's difficult growing conditions do not allow the grapes to ripen so they must add sugar to attain an acceptable level of sugar for the yeast to ferment. Wines labeled QMP (Qualitätswein mit Prädikat) are wines that did not require the addition of sugar to ferment.

Today, German wines benefit from very advanced wine-making technology. A few other special features should be mentioned. The wines of Germany tend to be lower in alcohol, somewhere between 7% and 10%. The labeling regulations are the most complex, but also the most stringent of any wine-making country. And finally, German wines are enjoyed before, between or during meals, the way Americans enjoy beer.

The major wine growing regions of Germany are as follows:

• BADEN: The southern most wine producing region. Most wines are made from the Müller-Thurgau with some excellent Rieslings produced and a small amount of the red Spätburgunder which is the German version of Pinot Noir.

• FRANKEN: Distinctively packaged in the famous "Bockbeutel" bottle featuring the round, narrow body. These wines, made from the usually ordinary Sylvaner grape, are transformed here into a refreshing, "racy" offering not duplicated anywhere else.

- MOSEL: Named after the famous Mosel River and includes its two most renowned tributaries, the Saar and Ruwer. These wines are primarily made from the Riesling and are arguably the finest in Germany.
- RHEINPFALZ: Between Baden and the Rheingau, this area produces very good Riesling and Müller-Thurgau, but it is the Gewürztraminer and the exotic Scheurebe which are its greatest achievements.
- RHEINGAU: The only competition for Mosel as the King of German wines. Almost exclusively Riesling-based, these wines reach a power and longevity beyond any white wines made on earth. Wines made in the top of the area near the town of Mainz have been reputed to live (and actually be drinkable) for 300 years!
- RHEINHESSEN: The largest area making pleasant and occasionally distinctive wines from the Sylvaner and Müller-Thurgau grapes. The finest wines in the area, however, are made from Riesling.

The following terms are distinctive to German wines:

- TAFELWEIN: The lowest category of table wine. Usually barely ripe grapes with sugar added to complete fermentation and should be drunk within its first year.
- QUALITÄTSWEIN: A quality wine of some distinction, usually with added sugar.
- QUALITÄTSWEIN MIT PRÄDIKAT: A strictly controlled wine which must be picked at certain minimum sugar levels and cannot have sugar added to it.

The following terms are the different levels of Prädikat wines:

- KABINET: The basic grade. Usually fairly tart, but can be excellent with food.
- SPÄTLESE: Wine made from grape clusters picked later

than Kabinet grapes. Has 1-2% sugar but also fairly high acidity. The impression is not as sweet as one might expect.

• AUSLESE: Same late-picking as Spätlese, however clusters containing unripe grapes are rejected. The wines are sweeter and fuller-bodied.

• BEERENAUSLESE: Made from riper grape clusters than Auslese. Very sweet dessert wine, but retaining the characteristic stinging acidity.

• TROCKENBEERENAUSLESE: Made from individually selected, late-picked grapes that are usually shriveled with Botrytis. A very luscious, and extremely expensive, dessert wine that can live for centuries.

OTHER COUNTRIES

• SPAIN: Has more grapes planted than any other country. It is third behind Italy and France in terms of production because the soil and climate generally produce lower yields than the other countries. Spain's superb reds from Rioja (made from Tempranillo) and classic wines from Catalonia (mostly Cabernet, Tempranillo and other local varieties) can rival any country's in all fields except recognition. It is best known for the unique Sherries produced in the southwest part of the country. Easily, this is Spain's, if not the world's, most versatile wine.

• AUSTRALIA: Began its forays into wine at about the same time as California. Even without the scourge of Prohibition, Australia lagged behind in the making of fine wines at the expense of inexpensive jug and "bag in the box" offerings. Its vineyard sites, all in the lower half of the country, are reaching their potential for producing as fine a wine as any other country. The Syrah-based wines, labeled "Shiraz," as well as many fine Cabernets and Chardonnays are finally getting worldwide attention.

• SOUTH AMERICA: Chile and Argentina have been wine producers for hundreds of years. The intense interest, especially from major French and American companies, makes one excited about what the possibilities will be in the next century.

• EASTERN EUROPE: With the fall of the iron curtain, Eastern Europe can now begin to upgrade and export many of its fine wines which have heretofore been unavailable to the Western world. It has long been known that many areas in Hungary and Romania are potential vineyard sites which could make wine to rival the finest in Europe.

CHAPTER 6

MAKING WINES

*T*HE MAJOR DIFFERENCE between the making of red and white wines is that red wines ferment with the skins and seeds of the grapes and white wines do not. Since the juice of nearly all grapes is white, it is the skins that impart color to the wine, as well as many aroma and flavor compounds. Tannin from the skins give red wine its astringency (puckery sensation in the mouth) which diminishes with bottle aging.

RED WINES

The juice of most red grapes is white and only by coming in contact with the skins can it change color. Otherwise it will come out like a white wine. In making red wine, grapes are passed through a "crusher," a machine that de-stems the grapes and cracks their skins to allow the pulp to come in contact with the yeast. At this stage, the combination of skins, seeds, pulp and juice is called "must." The must is then placed in a temperature-controlled fermenting tank where either a commercial yeast is added or the natural yeast is allowed to start fermentation. The pulp of the grape must stay in contact with the skins in order for it to pick up color.

When fermentation is completed the liquid is now technically wine. The mass of skins and seeds, called "lees," settles to the bottom of the fermenter. The clear wine above the lees is then drawn from the fermenting tank until all of the clear wine has been removed and only the lees and pulp remain at the bottom. This is called racking and is how most red wines are clarified before bottling. The wine may be further clarified by passing it through a filter or by use of a fining agent such as beaten egg whites. Egg whites, being positively charged, attract the free floating sediment, which is negatively charged, and together fall to the bottom of the tank or barrel. The wine must still be racked to a clean barrel or tank in order to keep it clear. This is the gentlest technique with regard to not removing any of the flavors of the wine, just the solid particles which can taste bitter and astringent.

If the intent is to process the wine as little as possible, regardless of any sediment that may occur in the bottle, it won't be filtered or fined. It is then aged, either in stainless steel tanks or small or large oak barrels. Wines such as these are made to age over many years, even decades. Within even four or five years of the vintage the tiny pieces of pulp which were pulverized during fermentation begin to attract each other to form sediment in the bottle. Unlike tartrate crystals (explained below), however, sediment tastes awful and must be removed by decanting or very careful pouring.

At this stage there are hundreds, maybe even thousands of choices for the winemaker. What kind of barrels do we age in? How old should they be? For how long? Most red wines go through another, different type of fermentation called malolactic. Instead of yeast interacting with sugar and creating alcohol and carbon dioxide (CO_2) by-products, a bacterial culture attacks the harsh malic acid in the wine (the same acid as on the inside of green apple skin) and converts it to lactic acid (the same as lactose in milk). This lowers the wine's overall acidity and makes it a little smoother and easier to taste. Malolactic (ML) can occur normally or can be induced with natural cultures.

When ready (a matter of months or years depending on the winemaker's desire), the wine is bottled and aged further before release. Aging in the bottle develops what is called "bottle bouquet," the final melding of the grape flavors mixed with the processing techniques.

WHITE WINES

White wines are made in a similar fashion except, in most cases, without the skin contact. After crushing, the grapes are pressed quickly to avoid contact with the skins. The tannic acid in all grape skins (red or white) adds astringency to the wine. This astringency in reds helps the aging potential. In whites this astringency may overpower the delicate flavors so very little, if any, astringency is wanted. Therefore, the pre-fermented juice is separated from the skins and seeds in a gentle centrifuge. The remaining liquid is placed in a fermenting tank or barrel, yeast is added, and fermentation begins.

Unlike red wines, white wines are fermented at very cool temperatures, sometimes between 50-60°. This is done to preserve the fresh fruit qualities and delicacy of white wines. Following fermentation, the new wine is clarified, then aged in stainless steel or oak barrels before bottling. Chardonnay and Sauvignon Blanc are occasionally aged for an additional time in small oak barrels to add extra nuance and complexity.

Fermentation of white wines is much longer than reds, usually requiring several weeks versus seven to ten days. During each stage of winemaking, great care is taken to prevent the wine from coming in contact with air which can "oxidize" it and cause browning. Oxidation in wine is best understood by comparing it to the oxidation that takes place when one cuts an apple, which turns brown within minutes, as do potatoes when peeled.

Two additional precautions usually are taken with white wines, but seldom with reds. You will hear the terms "heat stable," and "cold stable." Heat stability is nothing more than making certain, before bottling, that no yeast cells remain in the wine. If the smallest amount of yeast were present and the wine were subjected to even moderate heat, it might begin to ferment the smallest amount of sugar. It has been known to happen with sugar levels as low as .5%. Yeast cells are destroyed by heating the wine to 120° for 30 minutes, or passing it through a special membrane filter capable of straining out even microscopic yeast cells, or waiting until fermentation has completely stopped and all the yeast cells have expired. Most wineries choose the latter method since the heat and filtration process can remove certain nuances which would take away from the finished wine.

Cold stabilization is often done in white wines to remove excess potassium bitartrate, a natural substance found in grapes also known as "cream of tartar." White grapes contain fairly large amounts of potassium bitartrate. If most of it is not removed, the wine will form crystals when placed in the refrigerator. These tartrate crystals will either cling to the underside of the cork or fall to the bottom of the bottle where they appear to be ground glass to the uneducated eye. To remove excess potassium bitartrate before bottling, the wine is placed in a stainless steel tank and its temperature dropped to about 30° F. The wine is held at that temperature for a period of approximately two or three weeks. Excess potassium bitartrate will then crystallize and drop to the bottom of the tank where it is removed either by filtration or by pumping the wine out of the tank until the hose is just above the bottom where the crystals have formed. The "cold stabilized" wine is then bottled. Some wineries prefer to skip this step, feeling that the process detracts from the wine's flavor and nuance. Having the tartaric crystals appear in the wine means nothing more than it was not cold treated and, thus, may be of higher quality.

SULFUR IN WINE

Sulfur dioxide (SO_2) and its derivatives, mainly sulfite agents and potassium metabisulphide, is a wonder additive used in the vineyard as well as the winery. As an antioxidant, antibacterial and antifungal agent, SO_2 helps to keep fungus from attacking grapes before the harvest during periods of high humidity; it quickly and inexpensively sterilizes bottles, barrels and other tools used in the winery; and it can delay grape fermentation when there is a risk of it starting spontaneously due to a long trip to the winery.

SO_2 smells like the striking of a match; indeed, sulfur is what is used at the tip. When used in the wine to prevent browning, primarily in white wines, it can leave a residual smell which is unpleasant to many and intolerable to a few. Most white wines, if SO_2 is added, will house between 60 and 100 parts per million of sulfur. However, because SO_2 is a gas, it dissipates with time in the bottle and, with swirling, in the glass as well.

Beginning in 1987 all wines with more than 10 parts per million of sulfur had to contain a statement saying so. The law allows for the term "No Added Sulfur" but that doesn't mean that it is less than 10 parts per million. In the natural occurring process of fermentation, Mother Nature will produce between 30 and 50 parts per million of "free" sulfur. For a wine to not carry the "Contains Sulfites" statement, it must be manipulated far more than other wines.

THE ACID TEST

White wines may or may not go through ML (see earlier section for details on ML). If the total acid (TA) of the wine is such that lowering it would make it taste dull and "flabby," the winemaker may try to inhibit ML by either using sulfite agents or by lowering the temperature of the tank so that the bacteria which would begin the process naturally can't get started. In California it is legal to add acid, but not sugar. Since we have abundant sun, sugar is not usually deficient in California wines. As in Europe, the laws are adjusted to make life a little easier for the vintner. The Chardonnay/ML controversy among winemakers and consumers has to do with what style a winemaker wants and the winemaker's perception of what the consumer wants. A Chardonnay grown in a cool climate, with a long growing season, may develop enough sugar to ripen, but it will also have more than its share of acid. A cool climate Chardonnay, for example, could be harvested at 23 Brix and have a .9 acid. This is quite high and the resultant acid in the wine would be very sharp on the palate. A warm climate Chardonnay could be harvested at the same 23 Brix but have a .7 acid, a fairly moderate amount. The cool climate Chardonnay might benefit from ML by lowering the total acid and replacing the normally sharp malic acid with the creamy, buttery elements which many wine drinkers enjoy in their Chardonnay. The warm climate Chardonnay might not go through ML but, because of the lower acid, have the perception of more fruit, in this case the fruit of the grape as opposed to the flavors enhanced by the ML process.

Many people don't like ML no matter how high the natural acid is. Less than complementary terms like "green pea" and downright caustic remarks like "cat pee" have been known to invade conversations on the subject. It's a matter of taste, pure and simple. Some have it in their wines, some have it in their conversation.

Generally speaking, Chardonnays which do not go through ML are tighter and more shy of fruit than those which do. If a wine is well made (with or without ML) and comes from a proven vineyard site, it can age extremely well—for 10 years or more. This is not to say that ML Chardonnays don't age. Many do, but many don't. Their advantage is that they taste pretty good right away, allowing them to be sold sooner and thus bringing some income into the equation.

ML is not an either/or question. Many winemakers hedge their bets by doing "partial ML." That means part of the wine goes through ML and part doesn't. The decision could be based on the fact that even if all the grapes come from one vineyard, all the grapes may not have reached maturity at the same rate. Sun exposure, hillside slopes, soil differences or even a day or two difference in picking can have an effect on the grapes. The winemaker must make a determination as to whether ML is appropriate for some lots and not others.

After the wine is finished, including ML, the wine's numbers will be read again. The acid will decrease from the time the grapes were picked, unless the winemaker adds acid during the winemaking process (legal in California). Generally, a wine picked at an acid level of .8 will end up in the bottle at .65 or .7 total acid (TA).

Wine and Sugar

Once the fermentation process has metabolized all of the sugar available and has converted the sugar into carbon dioxide (CO_2) and alcohol the wine is considered "dry." Such a wine, red or white, will taste clean and crisp in the mouth because of its lack of sugar and presence of acidity.

Terms associated with wines that are not quite dry, sometimes called "off-dry," contain residual sugar. Residual sugar (RS) refers to a percentage of sugar left in a wine by arresting the fermentation prior to a wine becoming dry. For example, a Riesling may show some degree of sweetness, but Riesling is often high in total acid and has a low pH. Therefore, to attain the desired sweetness, sufficient to override the acid, a higher amount of sugar might be needed, perhaps 3% or more. The winemaker must determine how much residual sugar is desired prior to the end of fermentation in order to assure the proper sugar/acid balance. It is illegal to add sugar in California. In order for a wine to contain residual sugar fermentation must be stopped before all the sugar has been converted by the yeast. This decision is difficult to make if the winemaker has not worked with the same source of grapes over a long period of time. With a vineyard history of knowing how the wine should be made in order to obtain the desired results, the winemaker can be more sure of when to pick the grapes. After several vintages, the winemakers begin to get a handle on how their winemaking decisions affect the wine two or three years later.

Chardonnay is normally a dry wine. It is also expected to be full-flavored and possess some oak or "vanilla" components which are derived from oak aging. If a winemaker is dealing with a Chardonnay of rather low pH (and the resultant higher acid), the winemaker can stop fermentation between .4% and .7% residual sugar to give the wine roundness or fatness. This procedure could result in the acid level overriding the tiny amount of residual sugar and thus the wine will taste totally dry even though it is not. Intricacies of this type, determined entirely by taste, demonstrate the great skill required by a winemaker. Assuming fine quality in the fruit and skillful winemaking techniques, "balance" is perhaps the most important aspect of a wine today.

A Chardonnay with residual sugar is generally looked down upon by the wine trade. However, a list of the top selling Chardonnays in the country will turn up quite a few that have sugar above the threshold of what is considered totally dry. Is a wine great because its RS, ML, TA, etc. are viniculturally correct or because the consumer likes it? No book, this one included, can answer that question.

THE AGING OF WINES

Assuming that no outside demon interferes with the finished wine, i.e., faulty corks or bacteria in the bottle before it is filled, once a wine is bottled it enters into a different phase of its life. Because of the tumultuous act of plunging this liquid into the bottle at a very rapid rate, the wine "shuts down" in what is commonly referred to as bottle shock. Some wines like nouveau, or light whites, recover quickly, probably because there's not much to hide anyway. More robust wines, especially reds, need time to recover. Sometimes even a year or two must pass before it has the same fine flavors it had in the barrel before bottling.

As the wine ages, the flavors of the grape(s), the soil, vintage, winemaker's hand and such all combine to rearrange what you taste down the road. The small amount of air space between the cork and the bottle is all that is needed for this "reductive" transformation to take place. The interaction of acids, tannins, coloring agents and other compounds interact with the oxygen and change both the color, smell and taste of the wine. In most cases this is a positive occurrence.

The color agents in red wine begin to drop out and form fine sediment. This action makes red wine turn lighter and it begins to pick up brown hues. With advanced age it can become very brown. White wines, because they have fewer coloring agents, turn color faster, becoming more golden and eventually picking up brown colors with advanced age.

MYTHS AND REALITIES

A wine which tastes awful in its youth will taste awful when it's old. Too many people in the wine trade, from winemakers to retailers and the press, may extol the virtues of a very tannic wine with the saving line, "It'll age." The fact is, if a wine is out of balance, if the tannin levels are higher than the fruit levels, it will always be out of balance. Wines do not magically attain balance in the bottle. If the wine was too high or too low in acid to begin with, it will always be so.

The benefit of aging a wine (on its side so that the cork is in full contact with the wine to avoid air getting in and wine getting out) is the coming together of all the components from discreet and separate flavors into one complete whole. The vineyard, vintage, type and length of time in oak, the acid and tannin levels, malolactic, etc. will be apparent when the wine is young. As the wine ages, these components meld together to present one united front of complex flavors with the whole being greater than the sum of its parts. Each component ages at a slightly different rate and each has its own dominance in the blend of flavors.

Normally, young red wines from noble grapes are tannic and hard. As they age, the tannin and acid levels diminish somewhat and the fruit and concentration of flavors become more apparent. It is important to understand that if there isn't enough fruit in the wine to balance the tannins, it won't magically appear later because the fruit is also diminishing. If the tannins are overpowering, even with some softening, they will always overpower the fruit and the wine will never taste harmonious. Aging is not a panacea for mediocre wine. Everything has to be there going in or there won't be anything to get out.

What is the perfect age for a wine? That depends on the taster. The English prefer their wines (red or white) with considerable age. What a Londoner might consider a fine old claret, a New Yorker may find over-the-hill. It is as much a matter of individual taste as deciding what's a favorite white or red wine. Only by being exposed to wines of similar quality at different ages can you begin to get an idea of what your preferences are with respect to aged wines.

WINE STORAGE

Wines are hardier than most people give them credit for. While a temperature-controlled cellar is the only way to store wines for extended periods of time, most of us drink our wines within a few months (some within a few hours) of purchase. A young Cabernet, or other full or medium-bodied wine (red or white), can withstand fairly brutal punishment in a few month's time and come out relatively unscathed. As wines age, however, they become more fragile. A big, young Bordeaux, for example, would probably suffer no damage if it were stored in a Chicago garage for a year versus a temperature controlled cellar. A 25 year old Bordeaux would suffer considerably.

There are three important factors to consider in wine storage: temperature fluctuation, light, and movement. It is more important to keep the temperature constant at 65° than it is to have it varying, even over a month's time, between 50° and 60°. When the wine is at a constant temperature it becomes relaxed and settles into that posture. If it is cooled down, it contracts and allows air to take up the space where the wine was. If it is warmed up, it expands and allows the wine to escape and replace the air. This continual expansion/contraction of the wine allows air to come in contact with the wine more often, thus speeding up the aging process.

Light's ultraviolet rays will cause a chemical change in the wine, spoiling it in a very short period of time. That's why wines meant for long aging are bottled in dark glass or a leaf green that helps filter out ultraviolet light.

Air pockets will form if a wine is transported or moved about often. This can have the same effect as letting more air into the bottle through expansion/contraction. This is why cellars are normally cool, dark and motionless. Humidity is a factor, but not as important a one. Within most areas of the world no humidity control is necessary. Ranges from 50% to 80% are acceptable. Too dry and the cork will dry out from the outside in and allow air inside. Too damp and it's liable to slide right out of the bottle. As with temperature though, consistency is also the key.

A WORD ON FILLS

You may think that you're getting more for your money if the wine is filled all the way to the top with little or no air space left in the bottle, especially if it's an expensive wine. Unfortunately, the science of wine fills says that there needs to be some air space, about a one inch bubble when the wine is resting on its side, for the wine to breathe. If there is no air space, even the slightest fluctuation, a degree or two, will expand the wine enough to push the cork out. It could be a problem, although in most cases, if the wine is stored well, it will reach its proper fill level and stay there as long as there is no great temperature fluctuation, light or extensive movement.

CHAPTER 7

HOW TO TASTE WINE

*W*INE APPEALS TO FOUR SENSES: sight, smell, taste and touch. Each by itself is important; but the final impression is an amalgam of all four. Most experts pay more attention to smell than to taste, but the majority approach wine tasting to determine a total, overall assessment of the wine's quality or lack thereof. It is important to note that wine is a very subjective thing, yet the professional taster must be objective as much as possible. Professional tasters are constantly fighting their own shortcomings. A cold, upset stomach, personal or business problem can affect one's ability to taste a wine accurately. Moreover, everyone's tasting ability varies from day-to-day, even from morning to afternoon.

What we call the sensation of "taste" involves smell, the eye and even touch. A wine of brilliant color, for example, usually will score higher in a tasting than a wine of lesser brilliance, even if the latter is superior. Part of the subjectivity of wine involves one's "threshold," which is different for everyone. Threshold is the ability to smell or taste various compounds in wine at minimal concentration. For instance, one taster might be able to detect a very tiny amount of sulfur dioxide in a wine (burned match), while another taster will not detect it until the concentration is fivetimes greater. The former has a low threshold for sulfur dioxide, the latter a high threshold. One's threshold is different for every compound, and varies daily.

As with any flavor comparison, wine is very subjective. Professionals must be objective and rank a wine on its merits. It is very difficult not to rank a wine best which one personally likes. A good wine taster may rank one wine as best of several tasted, but drink a lower ranked wine with lunch because they like it better. Also, it should be kept in mind that many wines might not be particularly to one's liking on their own, but will taste extraordinarily good with food. In the same vein, an ordinary wine in a beautiful setting will taste delightful, while a great wine in poor circumstances may not measure up to expectations. For this reason, professional tastings are usually conducted under rather clinical conditions.

Understanding how we taste is very helpful. The greatest proportion of what we normally consider to be taste or flavor is actually smell. When wine is sniffed, the small olfactory, or odor-sensitive, portion of the nose is opened and collects information that is transmitted to the brain. Additional information reaches the olfactory regions when the wine reaches the mouth where it is aerated and warmed sufficiently to release more volatile components which are exhaled through the nose.

HOW TO TASTE
Professional tasters, whether they are in the wine, tea, cof-

fee or other trades, all use the same, easily mastered technique. While the technique might seem awkward at first, it will open a new world of taste sensation.

After observing color and clarity, the taster swirls the wine in the glass to aerate it, then immediately places the nose into the mouth of the glass and gives a quick, rather strong sniff. It might be found that one nostril seems more sensitive than the other, in which case the sniff should favor the sensitive side. If more than one sniff is needed, they should be spaced about 10 seconds apart, or more, to avoid overwhelming the olfactory nerves.

A moderate sip is usually enough to get the full impression of the wine. Swirl the wine completely around the mouth so it comes in contact with all parts of the tongue. Part the lips slightly, draw air through them into the wine to agitate and aerate it as much as possible. This procedure, though a bit noisy, is the best way for your senses to achieve the full impact of the wine.

Aside from the vital role played by the sense of smell, the tongue experiences the four basic tastes: sweet, sour (acidity), salty and bitter (astringency). For all practical purposes, these sensations are true taste, while the balance of "flavors" we detect in wine or other food is smell. This is why, if one has a cold which effectively seals the olfactory passage, food has little "taste" other than that which can be detected by the tongue, i.e., sweet, sour, salty and bitter.

A sweet wine might taste "dry" to one taster, while another can detect the most minute amount of sugar. The matter of threshold also applies to "sourness," which, of course, is high acidity and/or low pH. In a wine, the salty sensation seldom is encountered, but we do find "bitterness." Very occasionally, a wine might have a strong bitter quality, the result of excessive tannins. But generally, the bitter sensation is astringency, a puckery feeling caused by the tannins in wine; these dissipate with time in the bottle.

True tastes are perceived at various points on the tongue. Professional tasters learn these points so that they can separate tastes with more clarity. At the tip of the tongue we taste salty and sweet. Along the sides, the taste sensations are salty and sour. Bitterness is experienced at the back of the tongue, where some people are especially sensitive. The taste receptors at the center of the tongue are the least sensitive, but since some zones are more sensitive than others, it is important that all parts of the tongue are exposed to wine.

It is easy to evaluate a wine if one concentrates on what you taste where. If a wine is dry on the tip of the tongue, but fruity in the middle, it is dry, but has a lot of flavor. Some tasters confuse fruit with sugar. The fruit could be effusive in the middle of the palate, if there is no sweetness at the tip, it has no sugar. Acid is not so much tasted as it is felt. The prickly, curling sensation on the sides of your tongue is the result of acid. The gritty texture on the front of your teeth is tannin. If the wine is excessively tannic, you will also experience a bitterness in the back of your mouth. Try tasting wines knowing just this little bit of information and you'll be surprised at how accurate you can be.

One's taste, like smell, is subject to fatigue. For this reason, professional tasters seldom taste more than 12 wines at one time. Since the senses are keener in the morning, serious tasting is usually done then, although wine judges often taste for a period in the morning, then again in the afternoon, allowing a complete rest of the senses in-between.

The sense of "touch" is a very important component of wine tasting. This is the "feel" of a wine in the mouth. The astringency of a wine, as opposed to actual bitterness, is a matter of feel. You don't taste tannin as much as you feel its effects; puckeriness and a chalky sensation at the front of the mouth. The most important aspect of touch is the "body" or viscosity of a wine. Alcohol is the major contributor, but so are complex acids and phenols such as glycerin. Professionals will say a wine has "weight on the palate" if a wine has good body. A wine without body will feel "light" on the palate. Sugar is also a contributor; therefore, a sweet wine can feel "heavy."

The many acids present in wine make a vital contribution to its taste. It is the acid which carries the wine's flavors from the front of the mouth to the back. Esters, formed by the combination of acids and alcohol, are equally important to a wine's "aroma." Aroma is a term used in the description of a wine's vinous, or "grapey" scent. It is to be differentiated from the term bouquet. The bouquet refers to the smell of an older wine and includes not just the grape aromas but also the techniques used in making the wine as well as the vineyard from which the grapes were harvested.

Sauvignon Blanc generally has a "smoky" aroma, Cabernet Sauvignon generally has a "green pepper" or black cherry aroma. The overall smell of a wine, the combination of bouquet and aroma is referred to as the "nose." In organized wine tastings, a wine with a good nose, but some defects in taste, generally will rank better than a wine with no taste defects but a weak nose. This clearly indicates that tasters tend to place more emphasis on nose than taste, demonstrating that we smell far more than we taste.

Temperature is an important factor in tasting. A red wine served cold will taste far more astringent than usual. If served warmer, astringency will seem less apparent. White wines that are very cold will lose much of their taste and most of their nose; this is why professionals taste them at cellar temperature (55°). White wines are most refreshing with food when served slightly chilled, about 50°. Red wines should be served at room temperature, about 65°.

Memory is an important part of wine tasting. It establishes one's "platform" of experience and allows one to make comments based on that experience instead of thin air. Thin air, however, has not stopped many verbose wine connoisseurs from pontificating ad nauseam. Memory also serves to inform tasters what they are tasting. Once you've tasted a particular wine, or property in the wine, and committed it to memory, you will have an easier time identifying it the next time you taste it. This talent doesn't happen overnight. It takes lots of years and lots of practice. Just remember that no matter how good you think you are there is always someone else who is better. And, more importantly, you can always be fooled.

Don't worry if you can't identify a specific wine or even its varietal in a blind tasting. Even experts are often mistaken, and everyone has good and bad days. Furthermore, highly experienced tasters, when blindfolded, often cannot distinguish a white wine from a red. Therefore, no matter how well trained the palate, wine tasting is not a precise science.

In wine tasting, color and sight often are interrelated and announce a good deal about a wine before one begins the tasting regime described. In red or white wines, the glass should be held to the light and the wine should be clear and free from suspended matter. Its brilliancy often can be evaluated to a further extent by placing the glass on a white background and looking down into the wine. Color is best judged by tilting the glass to one side and paying particular attention to the wine's rim. If the rim of a red wine shows a purple shade, the wine is young or has a high pH. If slightly brown, the wine is older and more mature. Red wines can range from light red to deep garnet and even inky black. White wines should have some color, ranging from a hint of light yellow, almost that of straw and sometimes with a green cast, to medium yellow and light to medium gold. As a white wine ages, the color darkens and, eventually, will move toward brown.

Finally, as the tasting is concluded for each wine, particularly if many wines are to be tasted, it is wise to spit the wine as professionals do. This might seem wasteful, but it is the only way to remain clearheaded for other wines to be tasted. In casual circumstances, the wine may be swallowed. In that case, the duration of the "aftertaste," sometimes called "finish," is yet another aspect of taste. Generally speaking, the longer the finish, the better.

ESTABLISHING A WINE RANKING SYSTEM

In most organized tastings, wines are evaluated by an agreed upon scoring system. Usually, the higher the score, the better the wine. After the scores are tallied, the wines are ranked by order of preference. Many scoring systems for wine evaluations have been devised. Some (most notably the Davis 20 point scale) give a numerical range for each element in a wine. The wine is then rated on the basis of its final point score. Such systems are useful in directing new tasters toward paying attention to the various elements of wine, such as color and nose. However, it is important to note that if wines are to be ranked against each other, they should be of equal stature and varietal makeup. Judging a Chenin Blanc, Riesling and Chardonnay against each other would be an exercise in futility since these wines have their own unique properties which, for better or worse, couldn't be part of another wine simply because each one is so different. A typical Davis scorecard has been reproduced for your reference.

CHARACTERISTIC	MAXIMUM POINTS
Appearance	2
Color	2
Aroma and Bouquet	4
Volatile acidity	2
Total acidity	2
Sweetness	1
Body	1
Flavor	2
Bitterness	2
General quality	2

RATINGS: *Superior (17-20); Standard (13-16);*
Below standard (9-12); Unacceptable, or spoiled (1-8).

This system has fallen out of favor because as you pick a wine apart, you find that you give it a higher score than you think it deserves. It may be generally okay against the above criteria, but it may also be boring! Another problem with the Davis System, as you can see, is that no wine rated below an 8 is acceptable. For all intent and purpose, the Davis System is a 12 point scale.

The recent emergence of the 100 point scale takes the

Davis System to new heights of absurdity. The difference between a wine ranked 88 and one ranked 89 is impossible to explain even by the person doing the ranking. And again, a wine rated under 60 is undrinkable, making it a 40 point scale.

Edmond Masciana Wine Rating System

The Edmond Masciana Wine Rating System is based on two major premises:

1) All wines should be rated in their class, taking into consideration the variety and vintage. Chenin Blancs can only be evaluated against the best Chenin Blanc you've ever tasted, not a Chardonnay. Zinfandel can only be evaluated against the best Zinfandel, not a Cabernet. A young wine which tastes old is flawed. An old wine which tastes old is not flawed.

2) Since 80% of the wines available in the United States are commercially sound, the rating system should take that into consideration. This means that 80% of the rating system should be available for sound wines. A 100 point system that classes all wines rated under 60 as undrinkable, does not have room for the reality of the situation.

Our rating system is divided into groups around a 10 point scale.
An off bottle—0 Points
0 Points = Wine is flawed beyond drinkability through action by outside sources. Bad cork or bad storage are often the culprits.
A flawed wine—1 to 2 Points
1 Point = Excessive manipulation or bacteria. Sulfur, volatility, hydrogen sulfide or another bacterial problem.
2 Points = Same as above except not as excessive.

An acceptable wine—3 to 5 Points

3 Points = An un-flawed, but completely nondistinctive wine. Shows neither varietal character nor is it indicative.

4 Points = A good wine, some varietal integrity. Nothing exciting.

5 Points = A solid wine. Correct from the aspect of varietal and vintage. Shows some complexity and length.

A very good wine—6 to 8 points

6 Points = Has all the properties of a 5 point wine with additional complexity, several layers of flavor and a longer finish.

7 Points = More complexity, better structure and an integration of all the components like wood, fruit, ML and lees contact.

8 Points = Complex essences beyond the variety, but still retaining the varietal integrity. Lacking only the depth of flavors and a finish to make it exceptional.

An exceptional wine—9 to 10 points

9 Points = Nearly perfect in all aspects, except finish. A classic integration of aromas and flavors, married together to form a harmonious whole which is greater than the sum of its parts.

10 Points = A perfect wine. A wine which refuses to be swallowed. All the perfectly balanced flavors and essences linger for minutes instead of seconds.

TYPES OF TASTINGS

There are two major types of wine tastings: horizontal and vertical. A horizontal tasting compares one varietal, such as Cabernet Sauvignon, from a single year, but made by several different producers. An example would be the comparison of Cabernets from the 1993 vintage made by 12 producers. In this way, the differences between areas as well as the skill of the winemakers become clearly evident. The vertical tasting is one in which different vintages of one varietal (say Cabernet Sauvignon), all made by the same winery, are evaluated. This type of tasting shows the variances in vintages and/or increasing sophistication of the winery. A horizontal tasting would be 1993 Cabernet from wineries A, B and C. A vertical tasting would be 1991, 1992 and 1993 Cabernet from winery A. In either form of tasting, wines should be arranged in a dry to sweet, old to young tasting order or, more classically, no order and served blind.

There are many variations on these two basic themes. For example, wines can be tasted by regions. Red wines might be arranged for tasting in a light to heavy manner, such as Gamay to Pinot Noir to Cabernet Sauvignon.

CHAPTER 8

WINE SERVICE IN RESTAURANTS

*A*LTHOUGH IT MIGHT APPEAR RITUALISTIC to the uneducated, there are some good reasons for the wine service ritual.

After you've ordered a wine and it's been presented, inspect the label to make certain it is the correct producer, type, vintage, etc. When the cork is drawn, it should be squeezed to be certain it is resilient and, therefore, has provided a good seal for the wine. A hard, brittle cork is a sign (although not a guarantee) that air might have been introduced into the wine. Some consumers also smell the end of the cork that has been in contact with the wine. Most corks, however, smell like, well, cork.

At this point, a small amount of wine, an ounce or two, is poured into the host's glass for evaluation. If he or she considers the wine good and without fault, then wine is poured for the guests. The host's glass is poured last. The best wine glasses are clear, and of about 12 ounce capacity. They should never be filled more than a third to half full. The clear glass allows the wine's color to be observed, the low fill allows the wine to be gently swirled so that its aroma and bouquet can be fully enjoyed.

If the wine is correct, then tell the server to pour for the rest of the guests. If you believe that there is something chemically wrong, you should bring this to the attention of the server by saying, "I believe this wine is flawed. Would you mind trying it?" There is a delicate balance here. Rejecting a wine because it is flawed is quite different from rejecting it because you don't like it. If you are familiar with a wine and it tastes much differently than you remember, you are justified in returning it with an explanation. If you order a wine you are not familiar with, I suggest you ask your server for some counsel. If the wine does not taste like what your server describes, then you should reject it. The key to not making this a chore is to be sure of what you are ordering. If not, then ask the person who is selling it to you.

Careful attention should be given to pairing wine with food to create a "marriage" wherein the wine accents the food, and the food accents the wine, thus increasing the pleasure of both. Only by trial and error can this be honed down to an art. Generally, good wine matches good food. Color or country are secondary.

How We Got Here

From 1970 to the present, the wine market in the United States has enjoyed explosive growth. Sales of California wine have increased dramatically, but so have imported wines as well as those from other states.

Italy is now the largest exporter of wine into the United States. Italian wine sales in the United States increased four-fold from 1978 to 1985, moving from 6 million cases to about 21 million cases. Italy accounts for 60% of all imported wines, with France now in second place followed by Germany. Chile and Australia are making dramatic inroads and, more recently, so is South Africa.

Chile may have the greatest potential of all emerging wine producing countries in the world. Its soil and climate are exceptional. Add to that the millions of dollars being poured into the country by major producers, like Chateau Lafite's ownership of Los Vascos, and the possibilities are very strong. The only down side is the uncertain political climate. If things stabilize, it could usher in a new era of very high quality wines, not just in Chile, but all of South America.

South Africa was a major exporter of fine wines to the United States until the early 1970s. The political situation basically ceased all trade with that country. As things begin to ease up, more South African wines are becoming available and consumers will begin to experience some of the treasures that this country has to offer.

California wineries now ship close to 220 million cases of wine, whereas in 1970 the total shipments were under 82 million cases. A major difference is in the type of wine sold; almost 95% of all California wines sold in 1995 were dry table wines, compared to under 60% in 1970 when much of the wine was of dessert types. Because of the ever-increasing demand for dry white wines, well over half of California's table wine sales are white wines.

Studies have shown that 35% of the adult American population can be described as "regular users" of wine. The adult per capita consumption of wine in the United States is just under three gallons per adult per year or about 1.2 bottles a month. For comparison, in both France and Italy, the adult per capital consumption is close to 25 gallons of wine per year or about a bottle every three days.

However, both countries have experienced a decrease in consumption over the last ten years by more than 15%.

It was once thought that by adding up both the statistical studies and forecasts with the modern marketing trends, that the United States would become a nation of wine drinkers rivaling European countries before the end of this century. Stricter drinking laws coupled with health warnings and an older population base have slowed this potential growth to a standstill from what was once projected in the mid-seventies. More recently, the benefits of moderate wine consumption have been making news, especially with regard to heart disease. However, the laws governing labels have yet to allow any such benefits to be stated on the label.

How to Read a Wine Label

Today's wine labels are a blend of legalities, design and, occasionally, an indication of quality. In addition to the brand, the label must carry either a national (Product of France), regional (California), generic (Rosé) or varietal (Cabernet Sauvignon) designation. Usually, the finer the designation the better the wine quality.

One might see a label stating "California Cabernet Sauvignon." This means that the grapes could have come from anyplace within the state and the wine probably was a blend from several regions. Another label might state, "Napa Valley Cabernet Sauvignon," which means that at least 95% of the grapes came from this region (in practice usually 100%). Since the vintner is proud of the quality from this region, it is so stated on the label. Another label might read, "Chardonnay, Edna Valley, San Luis Obispo County." In this case, the vintner has isolated a specific microclimate within a region obviously considered to be of superior quality. Some wineries are cutting this even finer by including the name of a single vineyard. These wines are at least 95% from the area stated, but usually 100%.

"Grown, Produced and Bottled" means that the winery grew the grapes, made the wine and bottled it. Another term meaning the same thing is "Estate Bottled." "Produced and Bottled" means that the winery did not necessarily grow the grapes, but they did make at least 75% of the wine in the bottle (in practice 100%), and bottled it at the winery. Other terms like "Made and Bottled," "Vinted and Cellared," "Cellared and Bottled" and similar ones signify that none of the wine was made by the brand winery, but purchased elsewhere and probably only aged and bottled at the brand winery. This could occur if there is no actual winery, just a business name which contracts with wineries to make and bottle wine and put the company name (called a negociant) on the label.

By law, the stated alcohol level may vary by up to 1.5%, plus or minus. Thus, a wine labeled 12% might be either 13.5% or 10.5% by actual measurement. Finally, there is the vintage date or lack thereof. To carry a vintage date, a wine must be 95% from the year stated on the label. Since the quality of vintages varies from year to year in every wine growing region, this can be important information to knowledgeable consumers. Often, however, the vintner might feel a superior wine can be created by blending, say, 50% of a varietal wine from one year, and 50% of the same varietal wine from another year. In such a case, the wine would be "non-vintage" (NV) but that does not necessarily mean it is inferior to a vintage-dated wine. The vintage date refers only to the year the grapes were harvested, and has nothing to do with when it was bottled or released.

BOTTLES

The first wine "bottle" was probably goatskin, followed by the clay Greek amphorae from about 1,500 BC, and was used to store and transport wine until the invention of the barrel. The history of glass as a container for wine dates from the Fifth Dynasty of Egypt. However, glassblowing did not reach a point of any significance until the first century BC.

The first wine bottles were hand-blown, straw wrapped and round in shape and similar to the Italian fiasco still used today in Chianti. But the art of glassblowing for bottles was completely lost in the Dark Ages and, therefore, between about 500 BC and the early 1700s, wine bottles did not exist. The idea of putting wine in bottles, fortunately, was rediscovered and bottles became fairly commonplace in the mid-eighteenth century. Thus, they are a relatively recent invention.

Today, bottles are machine made by the billions and there are nearly as many distinct wine bottle shapes as there are wine producing countries. The German "box beutel," the tapered "flute d'Alsace," Italy's "fiasco" and the familiar soft and square-shouldered bottles for wines of the Burgundy and Bordeaux types reflect the style of wine they contain. The heavy Champagne bottle features an indentation at the bottom called a "punt." The punt substantially strengthens the bottle, an important feature when housing Champagne where bottle pressure is six to seven times greater than normal. The punt is also useful in collecting sediment in older wines, especially reds. The wine should be stood upright for a day or so to allow the sediment to fall to the bottom and collect around the base of the punt. The wine can then be slowly decanted into another container. Most of the sediment will be left at the bottom of the first bottle, assuming careful handling.

The "flute d'Alsace," also called a "hock" bottle, is generally used for Rosé wines, as well as some of the lighter white wines such as Riesling, Gewürztraminer and, occasionally, Chenin Blanc. The soft-shouldered Burgundy bottle type is used primarily for Chardonnay, Gamay Beaujolais and Pinot Noir, reflecting the tradition of the French region called "Burgundy," the area where these wines are originally from. The square-shouldered Bordeaux bottle type usually contains wine types from that region of France, *i.e.*, Sauvignon Blanc in white wines, Cabernet Sauvignon and Merlot in reds.

Corks and Corkscrews

For wine lovers, the bottle screw, or corkscrew, as it is called today, ranks as one of the world's greatest inventions. The first corks were tapered, thus easily withdrawn and meant only as temporary closures. However, concurrent with the development and widespread use of bottles for wine in the 1700s, it was discovered that wine would age to its advantage if sealed tightly with a cork as long as the cork could be kept moist by the wine. This led to the cylindrical straight-necked bottle we know today. But this type of bottle required some means to get out the cork, and it had to be a more substantial device than finely wrought silver corkscrews previously invented for removal of perfume corks.

The first patent for a corkscrew was issued for the Henshall screw in 1795. This simple device remains today and basically is an inclined plane wrapped around a post.

An improvement was made in 1802 with the Thomason screw, a double-acting corkscrew; still popular today. The so-called "waiter's corkscrew," generally considered the best today, was designed in 1883. Yet another type of corkscrew commonly used, and of rather recent invention, is the "ah-so" type. Rather than using an augur or helix to penetrate the cork, this device grasps the cork by its sides and works on the ancient Chinese finger torture principle in that the harder one pulls, the tighter the parallel prongs grasp the cork.

Corks are made from the outer bark of the cork oak tree. The best cork comes from Spain and Portugal where these trees grow very near the Mediterranean. Only the finest quality cork is used for wine, the remainder going to insulation, shoes and other uses. From the time it is harvested, by hand-stripping the bark from the trees, done every nine years during the approximate 200 year life span of these trees, the cork requires nearly two years of processing and aging before it can be used. Corks are slightly larger in diameter (about 1/8 inch) than the standard bottleneck, and most range from 11/2 to 13/4 inches in length. For a cork to furnish a tight seal against the entry of air to the wine, which can ruin the wine, the cork must be kept damp. For this reason, bottles, when stored, must be on their sides, or upside down as they are shipped from the winery. This prevents the cork from drying out and shrinking, allowing the possible entry of air.

The worldwide demand for corks has put a strain on the cork trade. As a result, corks have slipped in quality and incidences of a "corky" problem have increased tenfold. "Corkiness" is produced by a very small, yet incredibly powerful bacteria whose presence can be detected in doses as small as 1 part per million! If a wine is left on a defective cork for 6 months or longer, it picks up a damp cardboard smell and taste and is virtually ruined. It gets worse as the wine stays in the bottle and it cannot be removed. Estimates run from 1% to 3% of the wines being affected, making the push for a cork substitute more vigorous than ever.

WINE PRONUNCIATION

The following are wine names which seem to give people the most trouble in pronunciation, with Gewürztraminer leading the pack by far. In fact, the inability of many people to pronounce this varietal may well be the prime reason it has never achieved wide acceptance. This is a pity, because it is one of the most interesting of all varietals.

BARBERA: (Bar-BAIR-ah)
CABERNET SAUVIGNON: (Cah-bear-NAY. So-veen-YONH)
CHABLIS: (Sha-BLEE)
CHARDONNAY: (Shar-doe-NAY)
CHENIN BLANC: (Chey-NAHN.Blonh)
CHIANTI: (Key-auntie)
FUMÉ BLANC: (FU-may. Blonh)
GAMAY BEAUJOLAIS: (Ga-MAY Boo-jo-LAY)
GEWÜRZTRAMINER: (Geh-VIRTZ trah-meen-err)
GRENACHE: (Gren-AHSH)
RIESLING: (REEZ-ling)
MARSANNE: (Mar-sahn)
NOUVEAU: (New-Vough)
PINOT NOIR: (Peen-no.N'wahr)
ROSÉ: (Roe-ZAY)
SAUVIGNON BLANC: (So-veen-YONH.Blonh)
SYRAH: (See-rah)
VIOGNIER: (Vi-ohn-yay)
ZINFANDEL: (ZIN-fan-dell)

CHAPTER 9

THE ECONOMICS OF THE WINE INDUSTRY

*I*F YOU'VE EVER TAKEN A TOUR of a winery you've probably considered, like everyone else, how wonderful it would be to do this, live like this, etc. Not to dash your hopes and dreams, but let's take a hard, dollars and cents look at just what it takes to live life in Valhalla.

Being successful in any business today takes of stamina, hard work, savvy, patience and intelligence, as well as money. Probably no industry requires as much of these as the wine industry. It has many of the elements of any other industry, including one that very few could list, taste. Everyone's taste is different. There is no "right" or "wrong," only yours and mine. What makes the wine business fun, exciting and rewarding are the same things that makes it illogical, annoying, arbitrary and downright frustrating. Too often, a business decision in the wine industry is based on taste instead of sound business sense, and tastes are known to change.

STARTING A WINERY

Once you've decided that the call of the grape is too loud to ignore, you're going to have to make some very important decisions. These decisions may take years to unfold and, if you goof, may take years to correct. First, you'll decide whether you're going to grow or buy the grapes for your wine. Then you'll decide what kind of wine to make, how to make it and, finally, how to sell it. The chart below gives the average numbers for making and packaging wine. But, before we can get there, we have to build a winery. For the sake of argument, we'll have to make a few assumptions about your taste:

First, you want to make good wine that you can be proud of and charge a good price for.

Second, because they are the most popular, you'll decide to make Chardonnay and Cabernet Sauvignon.

Finally, you want to make a good living. (Make that any kind of a living!)

BUILDING A WINERY

It costs about as much to build a winery that can make 10,000 cases (each case holds 12 bottles) as it does to build one that will make 20,000 cases. We'll take the more ambitious number since we're not talking about the equipment that goes inside, where the costs can go up logarithmically, just the cost of the land, building and basics. Since you want to make good wine, you'll have to build your winery where the grapes grow best so you won't have to transport them too far. Napa, Sonoma, Mendocino, Santa Barbara, San Luis Obispo are all fine grape-growing counties. Unfortunately, the people selling real estate there already know it and prices are higher than other barren agricultural areas.

You'll need about 10,000 sq. ft. including winemaking area, barrel storage, tank storage and offices. This is pretty lean and basic, no fancy picnic grounds, underground caves, etc. Maybe you can do it for $1,000,000. You'll probably have to settle for some used equipment. There's a lot of it available. Some of it has hardly been used. Read on.

To keep it simple, we'll make 10,000 cases of Chardonnay; and 10,000 cases of Cabernet. Since we're using good grapes (either our own or someone else's) we have to spend the money to make the best wine we can. That means brand new French oak barrels at a cost of $600 each. Each barrel holds about 25 cases of wine, so quick figuring says 800 barrels for a cost of $480,000—or half of what it cost to build the winery!

Okay, maybe they don't all have to be new. Let's say we buy some one- and two-year-old barrels and only spend half that much (a mere $240,000). Because we have well-structured grapes, we can leave them in the barrel longer to pick up more complex nuances without getting too oaky. So the Chardonnay; may stay in the barrel for 8-10 months and the Cabernet for 16-24 months.

Uh, oh. If the Cabernet has to stay in the barrel for more than a year, where do we put next year's Cabernet? We cut our costs down to $240,000 for the barrels to house 10,000 cases each of Chardonnay and Cabernet, now we'll have to add another 10,000 cases worth of barrels because we need two years of Cabernet in the barrel at the same time. (Add another $120,000.) Fortunately, you can wait a whole year before you have to buy them. Unless, of course, there's a barrel shortage and you have to order them a year in advance and pay for them six months before you get them.

To recap your investment:
Winery Cost: $1,000,000
Barrel Cost: $360,000 ($240,000 for the first year and an

additional $120,000 to hold next year's Cabernet Sauvignon.)

Total: $1,360,000

Afterwards, you'll go on a 30% to 40% barrel rotation program which means that you will buy about 300 new barrels each year and sell off 300 of your oldest ones. You will pay $180,000 for those new barrels and sell your old ones for about $60,000. This means that every year you'll need at least $120,000 for new barrels sometime between one and two years before you can sell the wine.

Planting Grapes

The first part of this book started with how important the grapes are in the making of great wine. Can you put your trust in someone else to deliver those perfect grapes? Shouldn't you exercise total control over those grapes to insure their perfection? Maybe.

Unless you own suitable grape growing land, you'll have to buy it. The chart below illustrates typical costs of buying land plus planting and maintenance of the grapes. If you finance the project at low finance rates, your payments will be about $350 per month for each acre plus maintenance. A fully mature vineyard of Chardonnay will produce about three tons per acre of excellent wine. Each ton will yield about 60 cases, each acre about 180 cases. That means we need 55 acres. After planting, our Chardonnay vineyard will have cost $1,900,000 ($35,000 land and planting costs x 55 acres). If we finance it (assuming you can find a bank to finance the entire amount with no down), we'll be paying about $18,000 per month on the 15 year note at 8% interest. Did you say you had equity somewhere?

Our Cabernet gets better yields (4 tons to the acre yields 240 cases instead of Chardonnay's 3 tons and 180 cases).

We could get away with only 45 acres to make 10,000 cases. That will cost roughly $1,600,000 or another $15,000 per month with the same terms as the Chardonnay vineyard. By the way, you should find yourself something to do for the first 3 years since the vines won't be producing any grapes worth harvesting in that time. While you're paying out that $33,000 a month for your 100 acres of nonproducing vineyard, you'll probably have to go out and buy some grapes in order to have something to sell.

BUYING GRAPES

Since we've already decided to make great wine, we have to start with great grapes. Most likely we'll be paying top dollar for our Chardonnay; ($1,500/ton) and Cabernet ($1,200/ton). That means we'll pay $250,000 for our 166 tons of Chardonnay; grapes and $200,000 for our 166 tons of Cabernet to make 10,000 12-bottle cases of each. That's $450,000 for grapes picked in September which you'll have to pay for by March of the following year and you may be able to start selling the Chardonnay a month or so after that.

IF YOU GROW YOUR GRAPES

Typical per Acre Cost	Initial Cost	Yearly Payments per Acre
Land	$20,000	$2,200
Planting	$15,000	$1,800
Upkeep per Acre	?	$1,500
Total		$5,500 x 100 acres = $550,000/yr. or about $46,000/month.

You will need to hire someone to prune, weed, fertilize, etc. With 100 acres you'll get a better deal for maintenance per acre than if you only had 10.

	Cabernet Sauvignon	Chardonnay
Tons per Acre	4	3
Cases per Acre	240	180
Upkeep Cost per Acre	$1,500	$1,500
Debt Payment per Year per Acre	$5,500	$5,500
*Barrel Costs per Acre	$1,200	$1,200
Totals	$8,200	$8,200

*For ease of figuring we're just assuming you'll split that new barrel cost between the two wines in the same ratio that they contribute to the entire amount. If each acre represents 1% of the total, then it will receive a proportionate share of the expense. Since the total barrel cost of the 100 acres (after your initial barrel investment of $360,000) is $120,000, each acre uses 1% of its cost in barrels, or $1,200. (Cabernet will technically use less because the barrels are purchased every other year instead of each year with the Chardonnay, but we'll assume that the percentage of new barrels will be higher, thus evening out the cost against Chardonnay.)

	Cabernet Sauvignon	Chardonnay
Cost per Case w/Debt Payment	$34.17	$45.55

By dividing the total cost by the number of cases produced we can project a cost per case. The Cabernet costs $34.17 because, due to the higher yield, you get more cases per acre ($8,200/240). The Chardonnay costs more because it produces less cases per acre ($8,200/180). Once you pay off the debt, if you're still in business, your costs will drop by more than 80% in terms of upkeep. But, don't hold your breath. We haven't made any money, yet.

IF YOU BUY YOUR GRAPES

	Cabernet Sauvignon	Chardonnay
Cost of Grapes/Ton	$1,200	$1,500
Barrel Cost/Ton	$723	$723
Total Cost/Ton	$1,923	$2,223
Cost of Grapes per Case	$32	$37

We need to buy 166 tons of each grape to make 10,000 cases. Our total new barrel cost is $120,000. We divide this cost by the 166 tons to arrive at the cost of barrels per ton ($723). Each ton produces 60 cases of wine. You buy the Cabernet grapes ($1,200/ton), add the barrels ($723/ton) and divide the total ($1,923) by the number of cases (60) to arrive at a cost per case ($32).

PACKAGING COSTS PER CASE

	Cabernet Sauvignon	Chardonnay
Corks/Foils/Labels/Bottles/Boxes	$10	$10
Labor	$8	$8
Packaging Costs per Case	$18	$18

This is fairly standard for punted bottles and nothing too fancy on the label. We also are assuming that you did the label design yourself.

TYPICAL COST PER CASE OF BOUGHT GRAPES WITH PACKAGING COSTS

Cabernet Sauvignon	Chardonnay
$50	$55

TYPICAL COST PER CASE OF GROWN GRAPES WITH DEBT SERVICE AND PACKAGING COSTS

Cabernet Sauvignon	Chardonnay
$52.17	$63.55

These are "raw" costs for material and immediate labor only. Suffice to say that our wonderful Cabernet costs between $4.25 and $4.40 a bottle and our Chardonnay between $4.50 and $5.40 per bottle depending on whether we've supplied our own grapes or bought them. And, we've not paid for a few other incidentals.

These figures are on top of the initial cost of $1,360,000 to build the winery and buy the first round of barrels. If this amount were financed at the same attractive rate of 8% for 15 years, you would make payments of $156,000 per year. This would add another $7.80 per case of direct cost ($156,000/20,000 cases) until the loan was paid off 15 years later.

Is There More?

As you probably know, even if you've never been in business before, there are lots of costs one must incur that aren't on the tip of everyone's tongue until they start getting the bills. For the sake of keeping this book shorter than the Koran, we'll just list a few things and do a rough and dirty composite total.

Licensing, taxes, state duties (unless you plan on selling it all in your own state), insurance, utilities ($2,000 a month is average), trucks, office and winery supplies, etc. could easily add up to $250,000 a year for your 20,000 case operation or another $12.50 per 12 bottle case.

Almost forgot. Just because the wine is finished fermenting doesn't mean that you can go out and sell it. Chardonnay, especially a premium one, can't be released for one and sometimes two years after the harvest, Cabernet at least two and sometimes three or more years after harvest. Who's paying for the storage (all temperature-controlled) during that period? You have incurred debt from day one of the winery being built, and expenses from the time the grapes are planted (or purchased) to the time the wine is packaged, and you will not see a dime for at least a year after the harvest!

Unless you're going to do everything yourself from deciding when to pick the grapes, inoculate for malolactic, clean the toilet and buy paper for the copy machine, you'll have to hire a few people. Totaling up a meager wage (of course they'll work cheap, they get to be in the wine business!), workers compensation, liability insurance, social security, payroll taxes and such, you can figure for at least two workers and another $100,000 a year or $10 per case.

Are We Done Yet?

Well, yes. And, no. If we bought our Chardonnay; grapes for $37 per case, added the $25 for incidentals like labor, overhead and the debt on our original purchase of the winery and barrels, we're at nearly $62 a case or $5.25 a bottle. If we planted grapes, waited 3 years and are paying off our debt, we're at nearly $100 per case or $8 per bottle (not counting the 3 years of paying off debt with no grapes to make wine from). Now, the all-important question emerges: How much do we charge? After all this expense, sweat, 70 hour work weeks and time and effort, we gotta make some money. We'll double our cost.

Next question: How are we going to sell it? Do we have a mailing list of consumers who we sent an offering asking them to purchase our wine (nothing too fancy, we don't have any money). Are they going to shell out $11 ($132/case) for a wine they've never heard of or $17 ($204/case) for the wine from our three-year-old, unproven and unpaid for, vineyard?

THE TEAR SYSTEM

Most likely we'll have to sell our precious wine to a distributor who in turn will sell it to a retailer who in turn will sell it to the consumer. We sell our bought-grape Chardonnay to them for $120 per case. The distributor sells it for $160 to the retailer who in turn sells it to the consumer for around $240. The wine that we have a direct, no profit, cost of $5.25, ends up on the shelf for $20. If we're talking about our own grapes, the costs spiral from $200 a case to the distributor (if you include debt service) to $250 to the retailer to $360 for 12 bottles to the consumer. When was the last time you spent $30.00 on a bottle of Chardonnay? If it doesn't sell, you'll have to lower the price and your profit. It's enough to make you cry.

OTHER POSSIBILITIES

Obviously, not everyone in the wine business just got there. Many wineries have been around for generations, have most, or all, of their winery and vineyards paid for, but many don't. A lot of wineries cut costs and buy good to excellent bulk wine from an open and occasionally depressed market for less than what it would cost to make. Some have enough money to look on their investment as just that, and not expect the consumer to pay for that investment. They don't factor in their initial costs for land, planting and building. They also have more spendable money than you do.

Even if you buy your grapes, rent space in a large winery with excess room to spare (they're not selling as much wine as they used to either) and keep your overhead down to almost nothing, your Chardonnay will still cost you over $3 a bottle. If you sell it for $6 to a wholesaler who sells it for $8 to a retailer you're still looking at a bottle of wine on the shelf for $10 to $12 or at least $20 on the wine list. And, we haven't even talked about marketing, wine tastings, advertising, entertainment (the press and your wholesalers like to eat a lot) or any of the other parts about running a business that even the wine industry can't escape.

There have been tremendous strides in growing superb grapes at much higher yields than our model. Even if you increased the yield, without sacrificing quality, by 50%, the reduction in cost would only be $15.00 a case less for the Chardonnay and $11.00 less a case for Cabernet Sauvignon. This would lower the retail price of your Chardonnay from $30.00 to about $27.00. Big deal, huh? No matter how you slice it, this is a very expensive business. It takes a lot of time before you ever find out whether your venture is viable or not. When all is said and done, the consumer, the trade, the press and maybe even you will still have to stand back and ask: Is it worth it?

MASCIANA

GLOSSARY

ACIDITY: Grapes develop natural fruit acids (the most common being tartaric, malic and citric) which are needed to balance the finished wine. Acidity gives wine its relative tartness and serves as the backbone to a wine's flavor profile.

AROMA: In a precise way, this refers to the odor derived from the grape or grapes used. To be distinguished from bouquet.

ASTRINGENCY: This is a tactile impression experienced on the insides of the cheeks and gums. It is a drying, puckery sensation. The degree of astringency is a factor of the tannins coming from the grapes' skins and seeds and, in some wines, also from the oak barrels used for aging.

BODY: Another tactile sensation relating to the feel or viscosity of the wine. It is appropriate for some wines to be light-bodied (Chenin Blanc, for example), and others to be full-bodied, such as Cabernet Sauvignon.

BOUQUET: The smell of a wine that is a culmination of the soil and climate the grapes were grown in, the fermentation and the processing. Wines change in the bottle. Some wines develop "bottle bouquet" quite distinct from the grape aroma.

BRIX: A calibrated measure of the percentage of sugar in grapes and wines. Tests are taken to monitor amounts of sugar in the grapes as a guide to when harvest should begin. It is expressed in terms of percentage, i.e., 22% or 22 degrees Brix.

COOPERAGE: This term refers to any container holding and storing wine, from stainless steel tanks to large casks and small barrels.

DRY: The opposite of sweet in wine tasting. The detection of sweetness is an individual threshold experience, varying widely. Most people do not notice any sweet taste when the wine in question contains less than 1% residual sugar.

ENOLOGY: The study and science of winemaking. Winemakers are often called enologists.

FERMENTATION: A chemical reaction that occurs in the presence of sugar and yeast in which the yeast enzymes convert the sugar into roughly equal parts of alcohol and carbon dioxide.

FRUITY: A positive description for most table wines. It implies the wines are clean, fresh and smell as if they were made from grapes.

MICROCLIMATE: Used to indicate that the grapes came from a particular area which, along with the elevation of the vineyard and the angle of exposure to the sun, influences the outcome of the wine.

NOBLE: Refers to four grape varietals. Riesling and Chardonnay for white and Pinot Noir and Cabernet Sauvignon for red. Generally defines these grapes as special because of their natural tendency to make great wine without coaxing. Most vines, if left to grow wild, will produce more grapes than would be acceptable to make good wine. These four grapes actually resist the tendency to overproduce, inherently trying to make good wine naturally, a trait considered "noble."

pH: An important determinant of wine quality, pH is a measure of the charged hydrogen ions in suspension. Winemakers prefer a pH factor of between 2.8 and 3.4 for table wines. The pH is inversely proportional to the total acidity. A low pH goes with high acidity, and high pH with low acid levels. Low pH wines are more resistant to bacteria and normally have better aging potential. The pH can be changed with the addition of acid, which is legal in California.

REGIONS I-V (ZONES): This is a rough system used in California to help classify regions for grape growing. It works by accumulating the daily mean temperatures above 50° during the normal growing season between March 1 and October 31: the lower the total, expressed in degree days, the cooler the climate; the higher the total, the hotter the area. The system helps to indicate where the heat-sensitive grape varieties, such as Gewürztraminer and Riesling, would prosper over the heat-loving varieties, such as Zinfandel and Cabernet.

SWEET: One of the basic tastes we all experience. In wine, the perception of sweetness depends on the degree of residual sugar left in the wine and on the other constituents, the alcohol and the acidity in particular. Most wines containing more than 2% residual sugar taste sweet to most people. It is not permissible to add sugar to wine in California.

TANNIN: A compound derived from the skins, seeds and stems of grapes and, to some degree, from new oak barrels. The tannins, which make your mouth pucker, give wine longevity. Because they are fermented with the stems, seeds and skins, red wines contain higher levels of tannin than white wines.

VITICULTURE: The study and science of grape growing.

VITIS VINIFERA: An important species of grapes numbering about 5,000, but only about 100 to 200 of these are important, and account for most of the world's fine wines. Most of the grapes in the species contain seeds, develop molds and problems under humid summer conditions, won't survive freezing winter temperatures and are not much good to eat. They exist in general to be converted into wine.

FURTHER EDUCATION

The following is a list of books which address specific wine topics better than most.

• *Vintage Talk* by Dennis Schaefer, 1994. A fascinating, behind-the- scenes look at how wine is made. Interviews with the top winemakers in California.

• *Plain Talk about Fine Wine* by Justin Meyer, 1990. "Mr. Cabernet Sauvignon" tells us how the most sought-after red wine in California, Silver Oak Cellars, is made.

• *The Vintner's Art* by Hugh Johnson and James Halliday, 1992. In-depth description on how the great wines of the world are madeófrom the vineyard to the table.

• *Vintage: The Story of Wine* by Hugh Johnson, 1989. Takes a fascinating look at wine from a historical perspective, tracing its production back 8,000 years.

I recommend you investigate wine tasting groups in your area. If there isn't one, start one of your own with the help of a good wine merchant.

One of the best and most private ways to learn about wine is to drink it. An excellent way to try many wines from around the world is through the Wine of the Month Club which was founded in 1972 and still going strong after nearly 25 years. Write them for more information at P.O. Box 660220, Arcadia, CA 91066.